HAVE THEM AT HELLO

How the Best Call Centers
Crush Sales Projections

Tom Carolan & Susan Anderson

Have Them at Hello:
How the Best Call Centers Crush Sales Projections

Copyright © 2019 by Tom Carolan & Susan Anderson

TABLE OF CONTENTS

Acknowledgements

A Note from Susan

"Write what you know" is the standard advice given to authors. That's all very well and good, but sometimes, authors need to write about topics they know nothing about – at least, initially. That's when a good, old-fashioned interrogation session (or ten) comes into play. Bright lights, recording devices, and buckets of coffee all work together to extract a subject matter expert's in-depth knowledge and then distill it into text anyone can understand.

To be perfectly blunt, this book would never have happened without the patient "explain it like I'm a two-year-old, please" input of our subject matter experts. They say only a true expert can take a complicated subject and explain it simply. Clearly, Bill Cox, Matt Loker, Mark Coudray, and Nick Elser are exactly that kind of subject matter expert.

Obviously, my co-author Tom Carolan knows his stuff – it's his business, after all. I lost count of how many phone calls I made to him that began with the words, "Tom, this may sound like a crazy question, but…" They always ended with a patient explanation that not only helped me understand more but also left me feeling proud of his die-hard commitment to always taking the high road in an industry that's not always known for integrity.

Therefore, if there are strokes of brilliance in these pages, they came from the experts – people who've spent years mastering the complex field of ethical lead generation, either as lead buyers or lead sellers. All told, I'm proud of what we've created. It's our hope that you'll reap a nice ROI for the time you spend reading, and that what you find here helps you do your job better than ever.

INTRODUCTION

Looking for a better way to get more clicks, calls, and leads for your business? Don't want to break the bank – or any of the growing number of high-stakes laws now in place – in the process? No wonder you picked this book up.

In your role as someone who's working with a call center – either in-house or outsourced – you've got nothing but free time in your schedule. You had to find something to fill those hours.

Right.

It all started because someone figured out that Alexander Graham Bell's invention would be a handy way to sell products to prospective buyers. With just one phone, a salesperson could reach more prospects in a day than they could in a whole week of knocking on doors. With a bank of phones or a whole building full of them, a company could really move some product.

With the advent Wide Area Telephone Service in the 1970s, long-distance calls became a more cost-efficient possibility. With a call center, companies could expand their reach exponentially, selling nationwide. Once the toll-free number came on the scene, it opened the floodgates to profitable phone sales. You could call anyone anywhere in the country without spending a fortune. Even better, customers could call your 800-number to ask you to sell them whatever they saw in your company's advertisement.

Of course, with the huge flood of inbound and outbound calls that call centers made possible, what came next was regulation. It turns out that while people love to buy, they do not love being sold. They also don't like being called at certain times, in certain ways. The people spoke, and Congress took action in the form of laws that govern how companies' call centers behave. No longer was it enough to open a phone book and dial for dollars. Calls could only go to certain people, in certain circumstances, under threat of certain sanctions for violating the rules.

Technology has changed dramatically over the decades. With those advances, best practices evolved that make it possible for a company to walk the fine line between profits and penalties – but it's anything but simple or easy to do. With so many moving parts, it takes a sound strategy, eagle eyes, and a relentless commitment to continual improvement for a company to use call centers profitably.

Yet you're doing it. Every single day, you work hard managing humans doing a tough job. You've got to stay on top of scheduling, hiring, training, and sometimes firing them. They're the ones on the phones, but it's both your necks on the line when it comes to closing rates.

You crunch more numbers and hatch more plans than anyone would ever guess. You're on a perpetual hunt for the weak points in your companies processes and people, to identify then shore them up. Some days it feels like the boat you're all rowing is full of leaks to plug – with more springing up every time you turn around.

Yet, as complicated and draining as telemarketing can be, the upside can't be beat. Especially in today's technologically advanced world, there's no better way to make more sales than to get the right people on the phone at the right time.

Whether you manage a call center or outsource to one, you know that success starts with the quality of the calls coming in every day. Get more qualified calls coming into a team that's skilled and prepared to serve them and sales become easy and profitable.

This little book will help you make sure you're ready for calls, and that you know how to get calls that are compliant and qualified – at a price that makes sense. We've tapped the expertise of several industry leaders for this book, experts we are proud to call friends. Keep reading, and you'll get their best advice for making smart decisions to keep your company safe while exceeding your sales goals more profitably than ever.

We believe a rising tide lifts all boats. To be truly transparent, if after you read this book, it makes sense for us to explore the idea of working together, great. However, our bigger goal is to serve you. Digital Market Media is known for being extremely cautious while also eagerly adopting new technology and evolving marketing tactics. From this position in the performance marketing industry, it's our hope that this book will help you use the power of the phone to beat your sales projections safely and at the lowest effective cost.

CHAPTER 1

OPEN THE DOOR, SEE ALL THE PEOPLE?

"If you build it, they will come."

"Field of Dreams" 1989

"Liar, liar, pants on fire."

Every Business Development Manager, Ever

In the decades since Kevin Costner famously hallucinated hearing those seven words, countless marketers have learned the truth. Despite 1.75 million search engine results that come back on Google for that deceptively simple promise, it's likely that the number of people who've merely built businesses and flung open their doors to discover a horde of customers showing up is precisely zero.

That's why every business has a marketing department – whether it's staffed by a small business owner wearing all the hats for the budding organization or an entire team of employees tasked with finding and connecting with prospects to hand off to Sales. That's why there are more than 80,000 marketing books listed on Amazon. Likewise, that's why there are more than 763,000 marketing blogs on Google. The reality is, building "it" is just one small step a thriving business must take along the path to profitability.

The list of marketing strategies businesses can use to get "them" to come is ever-expanding. Some tactics work better than others in general, and their power varies even more significantly when they're applied to specific industries. Online, offline, paid, organic, social, inbound, outbound – the brevity of this list belies the bevy of more or less effective marketing options out there.

For some companies, the customer acquisition process involves little more than being in the right place at the right time and offering a product or service that's necessary for survival at a price that requires an infinitely minimal buying decision. The sole grocery store in a remote area would have to really mess things up in order to fail.

For most companies, though, customer acquisition is more challenging. If you're in charge of business development for your organization, you know what it's like to hold a job title not many people understand. The sales team gets all the glory for bringing in revenue. But without the business development team, the phone would barely ring. When it did ring, the odds would be slim that callers would qualify as solid prospective buyers.

Like magicians, the business development team seemingly pulls new ideal customers out of thin air. The sales team works their own magic to transform those prospects into buyers - but they can't create revenue out of nothing; it's the business development activities you do that give them what they need.

What Is the Business Development Team's Role?

There's a common misconception that business development and sales are the same thing. The confusion is understandable since both teams work hard to generate revenue for and grow the organization. But their roles, goals, and challenges are distinct.

Strictly speaking, business development (BD) is about extending a company's customer base, whether that means reaching a new market directly or starting and nurturing strategic cooperative partnerships to sell to borrowed audiences. In some organizations, it's a Business Development Representative who spearheads this expansion campaign. In others, it's a Sales Development Representative who works to find, reach, and qualify prospects before handing them off to Sales.

The sales team lives and dies by whether they meet sales quotas. But the business development team's key performance indicators (KPIs) include:

- How far they expand a company's reach by generating leads

- How many leads they generate per month

- The value of the leads in the sales pipeline

- Once they generate leads, how well they convert after the handoff to sales

Like in a relay race, after the business development team hands leads off, it's the sales team who carries those leads the rest of the way. It's up to the salesforce to further qualify prospects to ensure a match between what the potential buyer needs and the solutions the company sells. The rest of the sales process involves discussion of features and benefits, possibly a product demonstration, handling any objections that arise and processing the paperwork that completes a purchase.

The better the business development team does in generating qualified leads, the easier it is for the sales team to meet their quotas. Success in the business development process means the pipeline is full of qualified prospects who are ready to buy after some further discussion with the sales team. The quality and quantity of prospects in the funnel determine whether the organization will meet, beat, or fall short in sales projections.

A Winning Business Development Strategy

If you've ever gone fishing, you know how important location is when it comes to the day's catch. You've got to know what you want to catch, what bait to use, and where to drop your line. It's the same when it comes to lead generation for business. The name of the game is delivering enough qualified leads to the sales team so they can close them effectively and cost-efficiently. It's a perpetual cycle of identifying, connecting with, and qualifying prospects so the company can generate sales.

Identifying Ideal Buyers

Before the business development team can get busy generating sales leads, they've got to have a crystal-clear picture of which buyers the company can and cannot serve beautifully. This means doing extensive market research so you can formulate a detailed buyer persona.

Not every potential buyer's needs are a match. Not every buyer can afford what your company is selling. Finally, not every buyer is likely to turn into a raving fan who generates referrals or a glowing testimonial. Keeping the ideal customer persona in mind is crucial in filling the funnel with leads the sales team can convert effectively.

Connecting with Your Prospects

While there are countless strategies that work well for attracting qualified prospects into a company's sales funnel, some work better with certain products and services than others.

A short and overly-simplistic list includes:

- Networking

- Speaking engagements

- Referrals

- Content marketing focused on helping prospects get to know, like, and trust your company

- Offering free consultations, trials, or demonstrations

- Digital marketing, including tactics that result in clicks, leads, and inbound calls

The trick is catching those prospects at the right time - when they're actively looking for the products or services you offer. Will they respond best to online marketing? Are they likely to call a toll-free number to start the conversation? Or are they more likely to take the next step forward if they can just click a button to connect with someone?

Finding the best way to connect with them involves extensive testing and optimization. The "test and tweak" process can take time and most assuredly requires patience and a willingness to pay for a period of experimentation during which there is no guarantee of any return on that investment.

Qualifying Your Leads BEFORE Sales Gets Them

Even after all the research and testing that goes into identifying and connecting with your ideal prospects, your business development department is still not ready to hand them off to the sales team. There's another round of qualification that must happen first.

Just because some of your business development ideas panned out and created a stream of new prospects flowing into your sales funnel doesn't mean Sales should hop on a call with them. Phone time is costly. Furthermore, there's a cost associated with every call your team fails to close - especially when that failure happens because the prospects weren't even qualified leads to start with. One more round of qualification helps to ensure every call Sales takes or makes has the best possible chance of converting.

It's wise to qualify every lead to verify that:

- **You've got the true decision maker on the line**. You don't want to invest time speaking with people who will, in turn, have to try to sell your solution to the real decision maker. Qualify every lead to ensure you have the decision maker on the line from the start.

- **Your product or service is a match for your prospect's needs.** There's no point in using your sales team's time to discover whether it's a fit. It's surprising how often prospects misunderstand a company's offer. Better to find this out sooner than later.

- **Your lead has specific indicators that signal a good fit.** For example, if you're selling life insurance, you'd want to be sure your prospects have the means to make a purchase. While you don't want to grill your leads too early in the conversation, it would make sense to at least confirm that they have a checking account - a minimum qualification for being a genuinely qualified lead.

- **Your lead is ready to make a buying decision.** This qualification speaks to whether your prospect plans to buy sooner or later - and that they've either budgeted for it or that they have another plan for handling the investment involved. The sales team will get the best results when they talk with people who are ready to buy, not just gathering information for "sometime" down the road. Qualifying this way can also help avoid sticker shock when Sales makes an offer.

Business Development vs. Sales: What Do You Have to Show for All Your Work?

Once again, Sales may have an easier time of showing an ROI for the company's resources. "I took X number of calls and generated $X in sales" is rather straightforward. While some number of calls might require a subsequent conversation to complete a sale, many will close in that first call, yielding a clear and measurable result.

For the business development team, it's entirely possible that the work of identifying, connecting with, and qualifying prospects results in… nothing. Again, the analogy of a magician pulling something out of thin air holds true. Many pitfalls in the business development process could easily derail any campaign:

- **You could have a message to market mismatch.** People might want what your company offers - but not the people you've managed to reach.

- **Your timing could be off.** They might want what your company offers but the time and place where they learn about it isn't conducive to taking the next step. For example, you might advertise on a billboard and catch the attention of hordes of commuters who can't call on the spot or even jot down the contact information in your ad.

- **Your offer – even if much-needed – could embarrass them.** It might be one that's sensitive in nature, inhibiting prospects from raising their hands. For example, if your company helps people get out of debt, repair their credit score, or overcome an addiction, it can be tricky to generate leads. What works for selling a kitchen remodel won't necessarily work in this case.

- **You could reach a huge pool of the wrong prospects.** They may want what your company is selling - possibly even desperately - but if they aren't qualified buyers, your business development efforts won't produce sales.

There's an Easier Way to Do Business Development, Of Course

Rather than starting from scratch and doing all the work of identifying, connecting with, and qualifying leads, you could skip ahead to the part where you hand prospects off to your sales team to close. In fact, by working with a performance marketing partner, you can avoid blowing through a lead generation budget and ending up with nothing to show for it.

What's ideal about a strategy like this is that all the risk inherent in research, testing, and further qualification transfers to the performance marketing agency. They take your offer and your ideal prospect parameters and do the legwork of generating top-quality leads. You don't pay for the background work; you pay only for the leads that match your criteria.

Whether you want clicks, inbound calls, or qualified leads, a lead generation company like Digital Market Media can deliver them for less than you'd spend generating those leads in-house. In fact, it's not uncommon for our clients to see their cost per acquisition drop by 70% when they buy business development leads from us.

What You Need to Know about Buying Business Development Leads

When you buy business development leads for your sales team, essentially you can get as many calls, clicks, or leads as you want, whenever you want them, almost like turning a faucet on. But you want to be entirely sure you're ready for those leads before you start the flow. We'll address readiness next, but a high-level assessment must include:

- How clearly can you describe your ideal buyer? Demographics and psychographics are important.

- What life events, if any, might trigger a buying decision for them?

- When is the best time for you to have leads entering your sales funnel? Some offers are time-sensitive, and it makes sense to coordinate lead generation campaigns accordingly.

- What sort of capacity limitations does your sales team have? It makes no sense to turn the faucet on if there's no way your team can serve the prospects entering your funnel in a timely fashion.

- Which days and times make sense for leads and calls to come into your system? It's crucial to be able to specify days of the week and windows of time for calls to come in. After all, there's no use having sales calls come in when nobody can answer them.

Compliance Is Crucial

A quick Google search for buying business development calls or leads will show you that there are endless possibilities out there. Deciding which performance marketing company to partner with is more complicated than just choosing one that comes up toward the top of the search engine results page.

Compliance with today's regulations is absolutely critical to getting the leads you want safely. We'll go into greater depth about compliance in a later chapter – but it's so crucial that it merits this quick introduction. Safe lead generation means compliance with the following (and the list continues to grow):

- Do Not Call (DNC)

- Telephone Consumer Protection Act (TCPA)

- General Data Protection Regulation (GDPR)

To put it plainly, not every performance marketing lead company shares our staunch commitment to ensuring every single lead you get is fully compliant. In fact, in the lead gen industry, fraudulent leads are not at all uncommon. Some lead providers promise extraordinarily low costs per lead, then expose their lead buyers to astronomically costly legal sanctions. While there are legal ramifications for fraudsters, recouping your losses is nearly impossible. They simply close up shop for a while and then re-open under a new business name.

At Digital Market Media, we go to great lengths to help keep our clients safe as they scale. One way we do this is by backing each lead with a Trusted Form certificate or Jornaya Lead ID. These measures record and date stamp the exact moment your lead completes a web form, including their IP address.

Lead Quality: You Should Always Have the Final Say

Getting a virtual avalanche of leads does you no good if they're not qualified. In fact, there may be no worse way to waste your sales team's resources than by leaving them to field unqualified inquiries. But when you can send them leads who are qualified buyers they can close efficiently, so exceeding sales projections becomes easy.

All calls you buy from Digital Market Media come with a generous duration period. What this means is that your sales team gets a period of time - usually 1-2 minutes - to talk with a prospect to ensure a good fit. If it's not a fit somehow, you don't pay for the call.

Business Development Used to Be Hard... But Not Anymore

For many business development managers, their work likely feels like an exercise in futility, full of false starts that go nowhere. Their sales teams clamor for more leads so they can meet their quotas. Their own performance is judged by how well Sales can close the leads they generate.

If they have to do all the prep work involved in lead generation - or if they end up doing business with a performance marketer of questionable integrity - it's no wonder when it doesn't work. But when they partner with a lead generation expert who can deliver top-quality, fully compliant calls, clicks, and leads, business development becomes as simple as placing an order.

As simple as this strategy is, it's not time to push the "make my phone ring off the hook" button quite yet. There's one more important discussion to have first to ensure your organization is ready for the flood of qualified prospects that is to come. It's coming up next, and it's important. We'll share some solid advice from a veteran of the marketing world who's helped struggling entrepreneurs build the business of their dreams, fixing problems in a way that makes him a highly sought after business turnaround mentor.

CHAPTER 2

FIRST THINGS FIRST... IS YOUR CALL CENTER READY?

"Suddenly a thought came to Hans.
He stuck his little forefinger right into the hole, where it
fitted tight; and he said to his little brother, "Run, Dieting!
Go to the town and tell the men there's a hole in the dike.
Tell them I will keep it stopped till they get here."

The Little Hero of Haarlem
An American Fairy Tale

There's one problem worse than flinging your company's doors open with the expectation of seeing a crowd of eager prospects, wallets in hand and ready to buy, and seeing nothing but tumbleweeds. It's investing in marketing that works like gangbusters… and not being ready for that success.

Imagine having to explain to the powers that be that while, yes, you've achieved a record-breaking high return on the marketing dollars in the budget, there's nothing to show for it. All the resources invested in generating leads, like water leaking through a hole in a dam, can easily be wasted. Achieving a state of readiness before the call center phone starts ringing is crucial if you don't relish the thought of watching your precious leads seep into the mud because nobody readied a bucket to catch them in.

In an organization that insists on cultivating its leads in-house, there's a considerable ramp-up period between when the light turns green for the business development team and the moment when the phone starts ringing. There will likely be false starts during the test and tweak phase of lead generation. More than likely, the sales team will have such an extended waiting period before their first conversations with prospects that they might conceivably become thumb-twiddling experts in the interim.

But it's not like that when companies buy their leads from a pay per call partner. In this case, the work of lead generation is already underway. The testing and tweaking process has already been completed. Like an oil well that's going gangbusters spewing crude, the hard work is done and all that's left to do is to capture it.

Many smart businesses turn to Mark Coudray, Founder of Coudray Growth Technologies, for help optimizing their call centers. The really smart ones do so before pouring gasoline on the fire. Mark helps them hit their specific KPIs to optimum levels before they scale. Here's some of the advice he gives them.

Get Your Sales Process Nailed Down First

You need to have your sales process completely defined and worked out because without that sales process you're presented with leads you have no idea where that person on the other end of the phone is coming from in terms of some key issues. How immediate is their need? Does this lead need to be developed? What is their actual status? You have a very short time to analyze their situation, to connect with them at the relationship level, and then to deliver your sales presentation in such a way that it results in an order.

"I've run into many organizations that are very ill-prepared to deal with the lead stream that comes to them from whatever channel they're using. Pay per call is no different than pay per click. You're getting a prospect delivered to you. You need to convert that lead as quickly as possible. In the environment that a paid call is coming in on, there's already some qualification there but it needs to be maximized without feeling too pushy."

Know Your Numbers Before the Fire Hose Starts Blasting

Here's the bottom line: You need to know what conversion rate is acceptable. Does 25% work for your numbers? Are you looking for 60% or more? Hitting your numbers really comes down to the sales process. There are ways to improve the chances of conversion, and the more efficient you can make the entire system through your partnership with your leads provider, the higher the likelihood your conversions will be good.

Setting and meeting real target numbers obviously impacts a company's financials. But there's also a lasting impact on your human resources that extends past the quota period. The morale of your call center agents is tied directly to the amount of rejection they experience and the pressure that's exerted upon them to convert.

If you've got a system that converts well, that, by definition is going to reduce the amount of pressure that management has to exert on the sales team to convert those leads. It also lowers the rejection level of calls coming in and helps guard and boost morale.

From a sales management standpoint, it makes sense to do everything possible to reduce the rejection rate by determining the causes of the rejection. In particular, you want to address how your call center agents will frame their conversations in such a way to reduce the tendency for a negative outcome.

Start the flow of calls too soon and it'll come back to bite you. Even with the opportunity to get low-cost marketing to generate a high volume of calls, you can burn time and money in your call center if the team is not prepared to answer and convert those calls. While replacing wasted calls is just a matter of money, replenishing burnt morale is not so simple.

Improve Your Chances of Conversion, Protect Morale

When morale becomes an issue, your conversion decline compounds. That's because the expectation moves from closing a deal or converting to a positive result to expecting to fail. When you set the call frame with an expectation of failure you're just literally driving to that outcome. The mental state is so essential for success. Getting the agents into that positive mental state and having them stay there over the course of the day is a full-time job.

A major part of sales management is figuring out how to maintain that state of positivity in your team. More challenging for each agent is figuring out how to bring it back when you've had a really bad call. How do you bounce back when somebody's gotten really angry with you and gotten very personal? It happens all the time – the other person feels offended or feels like they're being manipulated or persuaded, then they throw it back at your agent on a personal level. The more personal it gets the greater the impact on morale.

Feelings Impact Financials

Let's say you lose people because morale takes a dive because you weren't truly prepared to start taking calls. Maybe your call center starts to have a mass exodus. What's the financial cost for having to replace multiple agents?

The financial cost really depends on the product that you're selling and how its price tag is. If you're selling a low-priced product, a couple hundred dollars perhaps, that's one matter. The stakes are much lower. But if you're selling a higher-ticket product, everything changes.

One call center Mark worked with had just six people handling high-ticket sales on the phone. Before management called him in, they were struggling. With the changes Mark made in optimizing the call center's readiness, that little team saw a jump of $1.2 million in just six months.

Momentum Works Both Ways

Morale is contagious; there's no question about it. If you've identified one or two toxic people in your call center environment, you've got to get them out of there. You've either got to get them out for more training or remove them from the environment. But you don't want them in that environment because demoralization can spread like wildfire.

Your vigilance begins with walking around and building relationships with your agents. Then keep the lines of communication open – both verbal and non-verbal. Mark always looks for body language.

"If I'm walking across the call center floor, watching people take calls, I'll just sit at the top and watch. In particular, I'll watch their body language during and after the call, especially if the call resulted in a failure where they weren't able to convert. Then I'll listen to the comments they make after the call. In particular, I'll pay attention to any sarcastic, snarky comments they make loudly enough for other agents to hear.

"I'll go back in and listen to the calls from that agent and just listen for their tonality and their delivery, the type of questions they're asking, the sequence of questioning they're going through, whether they're being compliant to the sales process we're working with, whether it's a script or whether it's a free form. Are they compliant with what we're after? All of that comes into play to determine what's going on.

"It's a fine line between being coachable and requiring more training and education. But it boils down to the attitude of the individual. You can train everybody all day long. You can be the best coach in the world. But if they're not coachable and their attitude is not responsive enough to get them back into the game, that's not a project you should pursue."

With experience, it gets easier to determine quickly whether any particular agent's deflated morale is salvageable. It's just a matter of touching base with everyone in the call center on a regular basis.

Ascend Beyond a Transactional Model

As we've begun discussing, when you have a call center, there's a certain amount of legwork that's got to happen before the phone starts ringing. You've got to have your processes dialed in and your KPIs chosen so you know what to measure as you evaluate your results. That preparation is a bit like building a machine. Once it's built and tested, that's when you can look at pouring gasoline into the tank so you can scale. That's the starting point.

From there, you'll find Mark's "Ascension Model" invaluable. The Ascension Model is essentially looking at your lead generation and sales growth differently from how they've been seen traditionally.

Most companies follow a transactional model of business. Let's say you need 500 leads per day. Under a transactional model, you'd go out and secure those leads today. You'd do it again tomorrow, and the next day, and the next, and the next, always starting from scratch to backfill your funnel with enough leads to make the sales that pop out of the other end of that funnel sufficient to meet or beat your quota.

The Ascension Model is different because instead of seeing each lead as a potential one-time sale, a single transaction, you consider your leads from a lifetime customer perspective. Consider the value of a long-term successful client relationship. That could last years or even decades. Everyone's heard the statistics and admonitions about how it costs less to market to existing customers and that they're more likely to buy (and to buy more) than people who've never bought from you before.

With a transactional perspective, each sale is "one and done," and you've got to repeat that sales process ad nauseam to hit your numbers. But where the Ascension Model changes everything is in the realization that the value of new customers moving forward is up to 125x that initial annual value… per year… if you can learn how to keep them.

The Ascension Model involves designing the sales offering and the relationship with your client with a long-term view. The first order essentially remains transactional. But after that, your development pipeline should focus on retention.

Rearview Mirror – Or Front Windshield?

As Mark says, "Traditional businesses look at the way that they're successful based on KPIs and financial reporting. They'll look at their balance sheet, their income, expenses, and profit. Those are the KPIs that matter most to them. But that's like driving a car and only looking at the rearview mirror." You're evaluating things that have happened in the past.

Now, if you consider lifetime customer value and begin to understand what patterns emerge as that customer grows with you, you'll start recognizing some important patterns. Document them, and you'll soon develop a set of more forward-looking indicators. Instead of driving on the freeway half-blind because you can only see where you've already been, now you're watching the traffic ahead. Now you can see when brake lights come on in the distance and slow down – or when the road ahead is clear and open, so you can pick up speed.

When you focus on the long-term with your customers, you begin to notice things. They say something, and you hear it. They decrease their usual order, and you notice. They wait longer between reorders, and you see what's happening. Rather than standing by helplessly watching your relationship deteriorate, you're on top of it. Now you can have meaningful conversations to help get everything back on track (or to help them another way if yours is no longer the solution that will work best for them).

This is a very powerful way to take the customer base you've built and extend it. You can still use the call center effectively. Just shift your gaze from selling them today to encompass more of a forward-looking perspective instead.

Sounds nice and good, but does Mark's Ascension Model work when it comes down to cold, hard numbers? Absolutely. In fact, he reports that with the 145 clients he currently serves, he's seen them achieve in just six months what it used to take them two to three years to accomplish. If that's not a significant acceleration of business that's worth exploring, what is?

Looking for KPI Patterns

Taking a longer-term view on your customer base also gives you more useful data that you can use to spot deviations and identify constraints, so you can take corrective action before there's a serious problem. For example, you might pay close attention to your average length of call time. With customers who've bought from you multiple times, that time will likely be a fraction of the time spent on the initial transactional call. You can start looking at call times and determine whether you're moving towards a higher value relationship or away from that relationship. Transactional calls are longer and require more objection handling.

In addition to paying attention to average call times, it's important to track the following:

- Conversion rates

- First call resolution (basically closing on the first deal)

- Attendance and tardiness rates

- Average answer time (how many rings before a pickup, how long are calls in the queue)

Those are simple metrics that are worth being quantified and monetized in any call center. There may be other metrics worth tracking in your business, depending on the particulars of your situation.

Control the Process, Control the Outcome

Among the clients Mark coaches through his courses, he's seen multiple millions of dollars of new business come flooding in – even with clients who would have described their businesses as "stuck" prior to engaging him. The success stories come in from a variety of businesses, some relatively small. For instance, one client had a relatively small shop – no call center, just two people doing sales. After 15 years in business, he'd topped out at about $200,000 in sales. Fifteen months into following the Ascension Model, he and his one employee had grown their sales to $700,000 per year. Another client went from $3.6 million to $7.2 million in sales with profits increasing from $125,00 to over a million dollars per year. Another came in with a revenue per employee of less than $100,000, and now they're at $350,000 per employee.

If small businesses can see that kind of improvement with just a handful of employees handling sales, imagine what could happen with the scale that's possible working with a call center. Within a call center environment following this model, you have the ability to control the process and therefore determine the outcome. It's about getting maximum results with the least amount of human resources and effort.

In that vein, when you're ready to buy leads and calls, the goal is not to bombard your call center with numbers. Instead, it's to get calls that will convert at a very high rate. That way, you and your performance marketing partner work together to lower your staff hours, increase your agent morale, and to reach a highly-efficient state.

Wisdom dictates moving slow and testing. Once you think you're ready for calls, it's time to start the flow and then optimize before turning the volume up. You've got to have calls and data before you can optimize – but you don't want to view the process as "set it and forget it." Instead, you want to adopt the goal of continuous improvement with KPIs that speak to a long-term perspective. Walk before you run, and once you start running, recognize that you're in a marathon.

The Best Baseline Assessment of Your Call Center Agents Happens in Neutral

Everyone has days when they feel really crappy and days when they feel like they're on top of the world. Their performance mirrors that internal state strongly. In a particularly low trough or on a rising streak, the numbers your sales team achieves may not be reliable predictors of where you're headed. It's most useful to grab your baseline numbers in a more 'neutral' state.

Aim to get a baseline of your sales team members' performance in a "normalized" environment. Do so when they're not flying high or crawling through a rut... they're just doing what they usually do. That's the best time to measure performance and then to optimize it.

Each type of call center is going to be slightly different, of course. But there are some helpful multipliers we can use:

- The baseline value is 1x. That represents about 80% of the activity.

- An optimized situation would be the top 15%, representing anywhere from 4-5x the value of the baseline.

- A highly optimized situation would be the top 4% of your activity when everything is pretty much clicking and it's working super smoothly. That value is 20-25x the 1x value.

- Reaching the top 1%, you'll see the most focused sales pros. They're in the zone, everything is dialed in and going great. Their results represent 80-100x the baseline value.

Under maximum optimization, that's when you'll see astronomical growth. By the time you reach that point, you've long-passed the break-even point and moved well into profit. Then, the profit potential is a multiple of 80 to 125. Whatever you'd allocated to cover your overhead now becomes available for additional profits.

In this state, your call center agents are in the zone. They're operating as a team. That higher value is a direct result of cultivating an organized and engineered lifetime customer value. You're generating much higher sales, the average sale is much higher, and the frequency is much higher. That's leverage.

Preparing your call center to take calls from prospects who not only become buyers, but who also become the kind of long-term, loyal customers likely to refer other business to you is a crucial first step. Get that dialed in, and you'll be ready for the phone to ring.

But call center readiness isn't the only challenge you need to meet to get phenomenal results. Next, we'll look at a factor that has the power either to get your team on calls with people who truly want to do business or to land your company in the kind of hot water that leads to nowhere good. Compliance might not be a fascinating topic, but it's one no company that buys leads, clicks, or calls can afford to ignore.

CHAPTER 3

THE THREE-HEADED MONSTER... AND THEN SOME

"Suddenly, where a small man had stood, a gigantic dog with three heads towered over me. I dropped the staff and stumbled backwards.

Cerberus looked like a poodle gone wrong. Wow, that's one ugly, pink poodle."

Pamela K. Kinney
How the Vortex Changed My Life

If this were ancient Greece and you were one of the hapless heroes on a quest, no doubt there would be an encounter with Cerberus in the cards for you. The three-headed Hound of Hades sure made reaching a goal challenging. In Greek mythology, one head represented the past, one the present, and one the future.

As a call center owner or manager, it's not so much the past, present, or future standing between you and the sales numbers you need to hit. It's a wholly different set of concerns.

Unfortunately, these dangers are anything but mythical.

Monstrous Head #1: Compliance

Compliance issues threaten to publicly undo any hard-fought wins you rack up… if you don't play by an ever-changing and growing set of rules. The downside is steep and crushing. Worst case, professional plaintiffs set their sights on you, resulting in a massive class-action suit the likes of which would force most companies to close up shop. In the best case, you comply, crossing every T and dotting every I. But winning the battle for compliance doesn't put you any closer to hitting your numbers. It just ensures your company doesn't get dragged through the muddy court of public opinion and flogged by a crippling settlement. Yay.

Monstrous Head #2: Quality

Quality issues might not look as menacing as the fang-bared head of compliance, but don't be fooled. While there's no legal cliff to fall off of, quality issues can have dire results where your key performance indicators are concerned. Fail to slay this "head" of the telemarketing beast, and your call center agents will spend their days like they're on stationary bikes. Sure, they'll be busy, busy, busy all day but by the end of their shifts, they won't even be one inch closer to the finish line. Suffer with poor quality leads long enough, and you'll have the distinct displeasure of watching your best agents stumble and fall into a pit of despair, right before they leave you for greener pastures.

Monstrous Head #3: Cost Per Acquisition

Even if you get compliance and quality under control, it's like the numbers are conspiring against you in your quest. Spend enough, and anyone can hit their sales numbers without veering off into the danger zone of non-compliance. But that's a luxury you don't have. Even if it feels like you're being sent to do battle with one arm tied behind your back because it's busy handling compliance and quality, you still have to win – and do so affordably.

We'll delve into each of these challenges in more depth in upcoming chapters. But they are not the only concerns you've got to keep your eye on where your call center is concerned.

There's also the matter of managing a team of people doing a job many people would rather gauge their own eyes out than do. Not only are you tasked with finding and training all the agents you need to work the phones – ultimately, you shoulder the responsibility for their performance. If they don't hit their numbers, you don't hit yours.

Ultimately, Success Rests on Call Center Morale

No wonder many veterans of call centers liken them to pressure cookers, chop shops, or even pirate ships. As Bill Cox of Hola Doctor says, "The agents are your lifeblood. If your agents are unhappy, you're going to run into an issue sooner or later. If they aren't talking to management, you'd better believe they are talking to each other. Morale issues will surface sooner than later."

Even when things are going well in your call center, that doesn't guarantee smooth sailing. No doubt you've seen what often happens when agents hit their stride and start closing nearly every call that reaches them.

Nick Elser of Donnaefinn Consulting put it well, "Running a call center can feel like captaining a pirate ship. Good closers know that they're good. They can come with huge egos. Any time, there could be a mutiny. They could just jump ship. It feels like you're trying to manage controlled chaos. From a marketing standpoint, everything needs to be seamless. You need to know where the ship's point is. You need to have your navigator plotting out the map, or you need to be a good navigator. You need to have a good map. And you need to have a good first mate, your CMO or Director or Marketing."

The problem seems counter-intuitive to anyone who hasn't donned a headset. To an outsider, it seems like the better an agent does, the better the call center does overall. But insiders know that's not always the case – at least without a skilled call center manager's involvement.

What sometimes happens is that great closers get a taste of success and want more. The challenge is gone, so they come in, close a few deals, hit their numbers, make their paycheck, and then call out. Maybe for days or even weeks. In a high-volume call center, this behavior can virtually hold a small company hostage. In many cases, the top producers literally control the entire revenue stream flow for a company. They control their own schedules and become practically impossible to manage, and the company puts up with this behavior because they grow dependent on these closers.

A few tips Nick offers to combat this tendency include:

- Be intentional about developing more than just a couple of talented closers.

- Keep on top of team building efforts to lessen the likelihood of closers going rogue.

- Don't just develop closers; develop good leaders who can look beyond themselves to build other team members' leadership skills as well.

- Don't suffocate your fronters; they're just as important as the closers.

- Don't be afraid to take a hard line with an out-of-control closer. You might consider holding back commissions, delaying them, or decreasing the amount of time your golden closer is scheduled. Drastic measures, but they'll get the picture.

Your call center's health depends on optimizing your hiring and training process. The heart of this training needs to lean on the idea of a chain of command. As Nick says, "It may sound old school, but there should always be a chain of command." It will foster a feeling of duty among your employees.

Spotting Pirates Early On

If you take smart action, you may even be able to steer your ship back on course by paying close attention to what's happening. Be on the lookout for closers whose egos are out of control. They do some things that'll tip you off to a problem in the making. Maybe they close a deal and walk away from the paperwork to go smoke. Or, maybe they take lunch before finishing their write-up, saying, "Oh, I'll get to it later."

Maybe they're questioning the floor manager or Director of Operations. They're the ones who always seem to have something to say... which is a double-edged sword. These same personality traits that contribute to their talent in closing can also make for an employee who's hard to manage.

When Nick consults with call center operations, the first step he takes toward identifying problem staff members is to sit with them for a week, unannounced. This way, he hears their conversations with their managers, watches their organizational skills, and gets a feel for their commitment to fulfilling their entire job description rather than just the part about closing deals.

- How are they with managing their files?

- How are they with finishing up deals or writing up deals?

- How are they with turning in paperwork and reports in a timely manner?

- How are they in response to the floor manager?

- How do they work with the fronters? Do they exhibit an appreciation for the power of the head start their fronters give them to make closing easier?

Whatever you do, though, don't get blinded by the revenue stream your top closers are creating. There's a certain level of oversight that has to happen to maintain a healthy call center. The importance of the chain of command can't be overstated. Without it, you'll have chaos. You'll see these closers march past the Director of Operations or floor manager to walk right into some C-level officer's office. Not only is this behavior disruptive, but it also seems to give everyone else permission to do whatever they feel like as well. In some cases, termination is the only way to fix the problem, if retraining isn't effective. This isn't reinventing the wheel; it's simple business infrastructure maintenance.

Lead from Behind

Your job isn't easy. Not by a long shot. The best results come when you're able to strike a delicate balance between letting your superstars run amok and clamping down so hard that nobody can be self-driven anymore. Instead of veering off into either extreme, manage from a position of leadership.

Nick uses the self-admittedly cheesy analogy of a wolf pack. The alpha male leads from behind because he's the strongest and fastest, and has a proven track record of fighting enemies, hunting, and protecting the pack.

It's the same with call center morale. Leadership should not happen from atop a pedestal; it should happen within the team. Rather than seeing their manager sitting with his or her feet propped up on the desk, bossing people around, the team needs to see a hard-working and diligent manager with a heart to serve.

It's Easier to Manage a Winning Team

Personnel issues aside, one of the easiest ways to help your team hit – and even surpass – their numbers is to take a page from baseball. A team's effectiveness in getting on base depends a lot on the opposing team's pitcher. If the pitcher's firing in curveballs that are virtually impossible to hit, it's going to be a quick half of an inning. But if the pitcher's lobbing in balls that hitters can smack over the fence on a regular basis, the score will rocket upward. It's all about the pitch.

The good news is, this is relatively easy to control in a call center environment. Higher quality calls with consumers who display high commercial intent? Those pitches practically reach your agents like they're in slow motion. It's not just your top closers who can hit them out of the park – any reasonably skilled agent can close them.

String several winning days together, and you'll notice some welcome changes in your call center. Not only are you hitting your numbers faster and more consistently, you're also doing less babysitting and more celebrating with your team. No longer are you in constant rebuild-the-team mode, your turnover rates drop because your team is happy – even proud – to work for you because their hard work is paying off. The less time you spend re-training or firing agents who aren't performing – or hiring and training new agents to replace them, the more enjoyable and lucrative your own job becomes, too.

Call center management challenges aside, it's time to discuss the three biggest challenges that come with picking up the phone. Beyond the comparatively simple matter of herding cats as a call center manager, the challenges we're about to look at have the power to make or break your year – and in one case, even to leave especially hapless companies shuttered for good.

As they say, "first is worst." We'll tackle the issue of compliance. Before your eyes glaze over at the thought of wading through a bunch of unintelligible regulations and legalese, don't worry. We'll make it as painless as possible. Besides, whoever said that "what you don't know can't hurt you" was an idiot.

CHAPTER 4

COMPLIANCE, SO YOU SKIP SWIMMING WITH SHARKS

"You have to evaluate compliance not as an expense, but as a money saver.

Sure, managing compliance takes resources, but it's nowhere near as expensive as the costs associated with a breach."

Paul Koziarz, CSI

The phone's ringing. That's great news!

But that knock at the door? You look through the virtual peephole and see a bunch of suits, jaws set and fingers twitching. The one up front flashes her badge. It's one of the FCC commissioners, flanked by an eager-looking attorney on one side and a small army of "professional plaintiffs" on the other.

They want to talk.

Apparently, there's a reason those calls you bought for your sales team were so cheap. They weren't converting very well, but at that bargain basement price, maybe you'd win the numbers game and come out with some sales after all.

At least, you'd hoped so.

But now, you know the problem is bigger than a humiliatingly low conversion rate. Those calls were anything but compliant with the current regulations. This is going to hurt.

It's a scenario no business development manager ever wants to encounter. Thank goodness this is a situation you never have to face – assuming you find out how to protect your company by only buying compliant calls and leads.

Discussing telemarketing compliance isn't much more fun than getting a root canal for most people. That's why, shocking as it might seem, we've encountered marketing department heads who can't tell a DNC from a TCPA. And GDPR? Just one more acronym that covers, at least from the perspective of a layperson, a whole new bunch of legal gobbledygook that nobody understands.

That's also why we were so glad to be able to pull in Matthew M. Loker, Esq., partner at Kazerouni Law Group, APC and Professor of Contracts at the San Luis Obispo College of Law. Matt was extraordinarily gracious about walking us through the simplest way to give you the information you need to know about compliance when it comes to lead generation for your company.

First, we'll look at which regulations are currently in play (plus one that's likely to ramp up soon). Then, you'll find out about some red flags you'll want to be able to spot as you buy leads.

Is wading through regulatory details pleasant? Not in the least. But we promise to make it as painless as possible. Plus, to be forewarned is to be forearmed. By knowing how to protect your company, you can save it millions in legal fees and fines.

DNC – The National Do Not Call Registry

"Put me on your do-not-call list, please."

Click.

That's just one that way consumers can stem the tide of sales calls they get. It took an act of Congress to give people some relief from the onslaught of unsolicited sales calls making their phones ring off the hook.

The DNC began in 2003 as part of the Telephone Consumer Protection Act, or TCPA. We'll dive more deeply into what's involved in more general TCPA compliance in a moment, but the DNC part of TCPA is a good jumping off place for this discussion.

Does Do Not Call Apply to You?

Do Not Call applies to anyone making outbound calls offering products or services for sale. There are federal and state regulations you need to understand, no matter what size company employs you. With more than 266,986,860 numbers in the registry, there are state lists, federal lists, a Direct Marketing Association (DMA) list that's been around since 1985, and finally, most companies keep an internal list as well, adding numbers to it when prospects ask to be added to it. What all these lists have in common is that you should never, ever call the people on them.

There are exceptions, of course. The rule applies only to calls to consumers. Business to business calls are not covered; neither are calls made to business phone numbers – even if they are business to consumer calls. Political calls are exempt, as are calls from non-profit organizations, survey takers, and creditors or collection agencies. Should a consumer do business with a company, any calls made within 31 days are exempt – unless the consumer asks to be added to the company's internal do-not-call list. Cell phones and landlines that are not on the list are fair game.

What's at Stake If You Violate the DNC?

Violate the Do Not Call regulations, and the Federal Trade Commission (FTC) can slap you with significant fines of up to $40,000 per violation. The Federal Communications Commission (FCC) will also get a piece of that action, to the tune of up to $16,000 per violation. On the state level, the fines vary wildly.

Just a few cautionary tales to keep you up at night if you're not on top of DNC List best practices:

- **Dish Network** violated the DNC 51,000 times from 2010-2011, resulting in a $61 million class-action lawsuit which paid out $1,200 per call. *(https://www. cbsnews.com/news/dish-network-do-not-call-lawsuit-eligible-to-collect-1200-per-call/)*
- **Alliance Security** (a company that sells home security system installation), according to FTC. gov, "made or helped others make at least two million calls to consumers that violate the TSR, including more than a million to numbers on the DNC Registry." The case settled with Alliance (and its owner, Jasit Gotra) receiving a penalty judgment to the tune of $3.4 million. Due to

the company's financial challenges, the court suspended all but $320,700 of the judgment. (*https:// www.ftc.gov/news-events/press-releases/2018/03/ ftc-charges-recidivist-telemarketer-millions-illegal-calls*)

- **Caribbean Cruise Line** made 12,424 robocalls to employees of Sears between August 2011 and August 2012, resulting in a class-action suit that left the cruise line on the hook for a settlement of between $56 million and $76 million. (*https://www. chicagotribune.com/business/ct-biz-sears-caribbean- cruise-robocall-settlement-20180724-story.html*)

In an ironic twist, Sears itself got into hot water in 2018 for violating the TCPA by using an autodialer that "dials incorrect or reassigned phone numbers" with a prerecorded message that call recipients had not agreed to receive.
(*https://topclassactions.com/lawsuit-settlements/lawsuit- news/848808-sears-class-action-alleges-prerecorded- messages-violate-federal-law/*)

DNC Compliance

Finding out which numbers are on the DNC is simple, if costly. According to DNC.com, companies that make calls into more than five area codes, if they are for-profit organizations calling residential phone numbers, are required to buy the Federal DNC list. At this writing, the list for the first five area codes is free. After that, the cost runs $59 per area code and more than $16,000 for lists covering the entire United States.

Ignorance is anything but bliss. Should a company elect not to purchase access to the DNC list, it "could be liable for placing any telemarketing calls (even to numbers NOT on the registry) unless the seller has accessed the registry and paid any required fees. Violators may be subject to fines of up to $41,484 per violation. Each call may be considered a separate violation." (*https://www.ftc.gov/tips-advice/business-center/guidance/qa-telemarketers-sellers-about-dnc-provisions-tsr*)

There is, however, a "safe harbor" against liability if your company calls a number on the DNC accidentally, provided the company can prove that it meets a certain set of requirements. Those requirements include:

- Your company has a written record of its procedures to ensure compliance.
- Your company personnel receives training on DNC compliance.
- Compliance is monitored and enforced.
- Your company also maintains an in-house DNC list (when a call recipient asks to be added to your list).
- You've been diligent about accessing the registry every 31 days and documenting that process.
- Any violating calls were made accidentally.

DNC Best Practices

Obviously, you don't want to use seeking refuge in that "safe harbor" as a risk mitigation strategy. The burden of compliance may be heavy, but it's unavoidable.

While the smartest move would be to consult with an attorney who's focused on telecommunications law to ensure your company's policies keep you on the right side of the law, here are some basic rules to live by:

- Never call a number listed on the National Do Not Call Registry.
- Never call a number listed on your in-house Do Not Call list.
- Always add people to your in-house list immediately if they ask you to.
- Never make calls before 8 a.m. or after 9 p.m. in a consumer's local time zone.
- Never robocall consumers who haven't given express, written consent for you to do so.
- Always transmit your Caller ID information – don't try to be tricky by using caller ID "spoofing" so your call appears to be coming from someone or somewhere else.
- Always seek to minimize the number of answered calls that get abandoned.
- Never hang up on a call without giving consumers at least 15 seconds or four rings to answer.
- Obviously, never threaten or intimidate anyone you speak with.
- Never use obscene language during calls.
- Never call with the intent to harass, annoy, or abuse consumers.
- Always synchronize your lists monthly by scrubbing against the DNC every 31 days.

*(https://www.ftc.gov/tips-advice/business-center/guidance/
complying-telemarketing-sales-rule)*

TCPA – The Telephone Consumer Protection Act

Ring, ring

You run to answer your phone, which you left in the kitchen. After avoiding half-tripping over the dog by detouring barefoot into the pile of Legos your child left on the floor, you finally reach your phone. Answering breathlessly, you can feel your blood pressure skyrocket as you realize all that hustle just went into answering yet another call from a robot offering to sell you a health insurance plan. Worse still, it's been months since you completed that online form so you could get information about health insurance. You've been insured now for a while – but the calls never seem to stop.

It's exactly this kind of scenario that prompted the creation of the Telephone Consumer Protection Act of 1991. Specifically, it was enacted to deal with the annoyance of unconsented autodialed telephone calls.

Prior to the TCPA, consumers were plagued by exactly this kind of call during dinner, at night, while driving – you name the time and place and they probably got assaulted by calls then and there. Consumers had had it up to "here" with this nonsense and Congress got an earful about it.

Back in 1991, of course, most of these calls hit landlines. Now, with most people using mobiles, a continual onslaught of calls is even more intrusive since our phones are always with us. The world has changed just a bit since then, but Congress wisely left some details of the legislation ambiguous on purpose where it relates to technology. Several changes to the regulations took effect in late 2013 – primarily focused on autodialing and pre-recorded messages.

The TCPA was enacted and continues to remain in effect to give consumers some sort of relief. Without prior expressed consent given by the consumer, and the level of that consent depends on what type of call it is (including SMS text messaging), companies put themselves in danger of fines and astronomically high judgments.

In a nutshell, the TCPA lays out rules for companies that use autodialing and/or pre-recorded marketing messages, whether the company is calling residential or mobile numbers. A company has to provide a "clear and conspicuous" disclosure to consenting consumers that:

- They may receive telemarketing calls that may be initiated by an autodialer and may come in the form of a pre-recorded message (also called an artificial voice).
- The consumer consents to be called on a specific phone number.

- The consumer does not have to provide this consent in order to buy the company's products or services.

Does TCPA Apply to You?

The list of organizations and purposes that are not subject to the TCPA is short:

1. If you're making debt collection calls, you're in the clear for TCPA, although you've got other regulations to follow (see the Fair Debt Collection Practices Act).
2. If you're calling voters and prospective voters for political or campaign-related purposes manually, you're fine. If you're using an autodialer or pre-recorded message to call or text, you'll want to heed the Enforcement Advisory of March 14, 2016, and you'll need to get prior express consent from the people you call. *(https://www.wileyrein.com/ newsroom-newsletters-item-FCC-Issues-Enforcement-Advisory-Reminding-Political-Campaigns-Calling-Texting-Restrictions-TCPA.html)*
3. If you're calling for the purpose of taking a survey or doing research, you're fine. Obviously, don't try to sneak a sales call or solicitation in there.
4. If your call is purely informational in nature, like when your credit card company calls with a fraud alert, your child's school calls to say your child was absent, your cell phone company contacts you to let you know you've gone way over your data allotment,

or the florist calls to say those roses you ordered have been delivered… that kind of call is fine.

Mix any of those call types with a marketing message, and you're back to telemarketing and all the regulations that entails.

If you're reading this book, that's a pretty good sign that your company is legally obligated to know, understand, and comply with the TCPA. Any company that does the following should pay attention to the TCPA, get prior written consent, and direct specific questions to an attorney experienced in this area of the law:

- If you call residential phones using a pre-recorded message or artificial voice
- If you call mobile numbers using a pre-recorded message, artificial voice, or an automatic dialing system
- If you call mobile numbers for marketing purposes, or residential numbers for any of the purposes listed above

Dangerous TCPA Myths

From the most glaring and alarming errors to some more common misconceptions, at Digital Market Media, we've heard it all. Here are some of the ways that companies put themselves in peril by not understanding the TCPA.

- *The TCPA is the same as the DNC… right?*
  Yes, for real, we hear that one! No. The DNC is part of the TCPA; you can't just comply with the DNC and call it good.
- *We're only calling B2B, so the TCPA doesn't apply.*
  Not exactly. If your company calls wireless numbers using an automatic telephone dialing system (ATDS), you've got to have prior consent.
- *But we're calling for some reason other than sales.*
  Sorry, if you're calling a wireless number, even to take a survey or to provide information, you need prior express written consent to use an autodialer.
- *It's not really a wireless number if it's ported from a landline.*
  There's an app for that, and you're still responsible here. There's a service called Neustar that'll identify phone numbers that fall into this category. You'll want to update your list every 15 days to ensure you stay safely in the grace period; beyond that, you risk being in violation and subject to fines.
- *We can't help it if someone on our list changed wireless phone numbers.*
  The regulations cover that, too. You can call a reassigned number only once before you're in danger. It might sound crazy, but the responsibility to identify and remove wireless numbers that switch hands falls on the company – not the consumer.
- *We don't have to worry about TCPA because we use a third party to make our calls.*
  Telemarketing companies might try to tell you that you're in the clear, that they'll take the brunt of any

complaints that get filed, and that they've got you covered. Believe that pack of lies at your own risk. You're still on the hook, even if your call center is not making the calls in-house. The burden of monitoring calls for compliance falls to you, whether you audit call records, listen to recordings, or walk the floors of the call centers you hire. This is just one good reason to scrutinize and vet anyone you partner with on your telemarketing efforts.

- *We can just give people the opportunity to speak with the next available agent to be added to our in-house Do Not Call list. That'll cover our "consent" bases.*
No, no, no. A thousand times no! Yes, you need an Abandoned Call Message in case there's a gap longer than two seconds between the moment someone answers the number your autodialer calls and the moment when the call connects with a live agent. In fact, if your abandon rate exceeds 3% in a 30-day period, you've got a legal problem brewing. That message must give people who answer your calls the option to push a button to be added to your in-house Do Not Call list. You can't make them talk to a live agent before they can get off your list.

- *We're covered. We only use text (SMS) messages, not calls.*
Sorry, the FCC sees phone calls and text messages as the same under the TCPA regulations.

- *We paid good money for this list. By golly, we're calling it!*
If you buy and use a list, the list becomes yours in the eyes of the law. Are you really sure it's a safe list from a vendor you can trust? Sunk costs aside, the

risks involved in calling a questionable list can be astronomical.

- *We start each call asking for consent.*
  You're asking for trouble! Prior written consent means you got consent in writing before you made the call. Don't have it? You'd better either scrap those numbers or call them manually rather than using any form of autodialer.

What's at Stake If You Violate the TCPA?

"We are pleased to resolve this matter," the Bank of America spokesperson said. No doubt, the bank was eager to put this class-action suit behind them. The $32 million payout was going to hurt, but at a potential $11,000 fine per violation, they may have gotten off easy by settling for that astronomical sum. Bank of America's no mom and pop shop, so this suit wasn't quite enough to bankrupt them. But while this 2013 settlement may have been the largest payout in TCPA history at the time, it ought to serve as a cautionary tale for companies that would have to close up shop if they faced similar sanctions. *(http://www.kleinmoynihan.com/record-breaking-tcpa-class-action-settlement/)*

Here are some similarly spine-tingling tales of woe:

- **American Express** used an autodialer without getting prior express written consent. They contracted with a third-party telemarketing company, Alorica, Inc. for nearly seven years to call prospective customers for the purposes of getting them to sign up for a small business credit card. Amex tried to foist responsibility off on Alorica but ended up settling the class-action suit to the tune of $8.25 million, which included plaintiff attorney fees of over $3 million. Outsourcing does not shield you from legal responsibility. If you – or your telemarketing vendor – use autodialing technology, you've got to have prior express written consent from the people getting these calls.

- **Sirius XM** dropped the ball in a few ways in this case, including failure to manage their DNC list, improper use of autodialers, and "vicarious liability" stemming from outsourcing to a telemarketing company. The case that sparked the legal challenges happened because the plaintiff bought a car that came equipped with a trial subscription to Sirius XM. As his trial period came to a close, he started getting autodialed calls on his cellphone after 9 p.m. trying to get him to subscribe to the service. He asked to be put on the DNC list, but it didn't happen. For nearly eight years, this kind of telemarketing mismanagement went on. In the end, Sirius XM Radio, Inc. coughed up $35 million to establish a settlement fund to satisfy a growing number of class-action suits.

- **iHeartMedia** seemed to think they'd beaten the system and figured out a way to use SMS for marketing without getting prior express written consent. It did not go well for them, to say the least. Their radio stations encouraged listeners to text in their song requests or to enter contests using SMS. That would have been fine if the only response iHeartMedia sent back was "Thanks. We got your message." But instead, they sent back texts containing marketing messages. The lawyers involved had a nice payday – about $3.4 million. The company set up a settlement fund of $8.5 million. The courts treat text messages as if they were phone calls; you've simply got to have prior express written consent, or face liability of up to $1,500 per text.

- **Wells Fargo** also dropped the ball where prior express consent is concerned between 2011 and 2016. Wells Fargo denies wrongdoing in the charges – autodialing customers on their cell phones to pitch mortgages and home equity loans. To avoid the expenses of going to trial, the company agreed to settle the lawsuit by paying in excess of $16.3 million. It would have certainly been a lot cheaper just to scrub their list of cell numbers and to ensure they had prior express written consent.
- **State Farm** rounds out this small list of big penalties with a $7 million settlement they had to pay because the telemarketing company they hired, Variable Marketing, to call consumers who might want to buy insurance violated compliance laws. Legal responsibility does not evaporate when you sign on the dotted line with a vendor.

Skirting the TCPA with Technology… Maybe

There is some confusion in the marketplace concerning what type of technologies are allowed and not allowed. For example, there is a technology that requires a click to dial. It's done one at a time and it's not actually using your finger to dial the number out but it's clicking on that number to dial a consumer.

As Matt Loker says, "Things get really, really, muddy in that regard. What we really focus on when regarding new technologies what the intent of the statute is. Congress enacted the statute specifically to address the problem of these auto-dialed phone calls. What's going to be subject to the law is going to be a case by case decision.

"Previously, before the FCC got involved just recently, by the BP circuit court of appeal in the FCC, what we're seeing is a predictive dialer be subject to the statute, sometimes pre-dialing will be subject to the statute, and they looked at how do these dialers function? Are they placing a lot of calls simultaneously? Is there any sort of human interaction or intervention to place those calls?"

Courts, as seen in Marks vs. Crunch, a decision that came down from the 9th Circuit Court of Appeals, are increasingly cutting through all the technical minutia to say that basically, any system that dials numbers from a list is a predictive dialer and is subject to TCPA regulations. It's a clear win for consumers and an escalated headache for companies.

From the corporate end, the focus has been algorithms, drop rates, and abandonment rates. From the consumer's point of view, it's just way too many calls with no consent. The long and short of it all is you MUST have prior expressed written consent. No matter what technological advances come down the pike in the world of telemarketing, the law will always come back to scrutinize how you answer the consent question.

TCPA Compliance

Boiled down to its essence, the TCPA regulations cover three general questions:

1. Does the phone equipment you use (or that your telemarketing partner uses) qualify as an automatic telephone dialing system (ATDS)?
2. Do you have prior express written consent?
3. Are your calls for telemarketing purposes or just to convey information?

As mentioned, the DNC rules fall under the TCPA umbrella. TCPA compliance laws are detailed and numerous, so the smart move is to engage an attorney who specializes in this area of the law to ensure your company is not engaging in practices that will land you on the wrong side of a courtroom. Some areas to focus on include:

- Be careful about calling wireless numbers with an automatic telephone dialing system (ATDS). You need prior express written consent. What constitutes an ATDS can be boiled down to any equipment with the capacity to call numbers it stores or generates randomly.

- Text messaging is the same as calling on a phone, under the law.
- Never, ever call numbers used for emergency purposes only (911, poison control centers, fire or police departments, or even hospitals or medical offices).
- Don't call fax machine numbers or more than one phone number at the same time at a business.
- Make it easy for people to opt out of calls.
- Get prior express written consent, which means:
  o It's in writing.
  o It's signed by the consumer (electronic signature is fine).
  o The consumer specifically gives permission for the company to contact them for marketing purposes.
  o It clearly specifies that the consumer agrees to calls that originate from an ATDS and/or that feature a pre-recorded message or artificial voice.
  o It covers a specific phone number for that consumer.
  o The language specifies that consumers don't have to sign the agreement in order to purchase products or services from the company.

TCPA Best Practices

In an increasingly litigious world, doing your best to treat people right isn't enough. Compliance isn't simply a matter of only calling people who want sales calls and steering clear of the others. Protecting your company from potentially colossal class-action lawsuits comes down to knowing, understanding, and documenting your adherence with the law.

Get It In Writing

For starters, you'll want to create and maintain a written company-wide policy that you can whip out on-demand regarding how you keep your in-house DNC list. It's not enough to write this policy and hang it on the wall in a frame. You'll want to train your personnel regularly on how to use it, and document that training while you're at it. Anytime you call someone who asks to be added to your DNC list, you need to record that person's name and phone number and remove them from your list within 30 days. You also need to keep a record of these DNC requests for five years.

Steer Clear

Don't ever call or text people before 8:00 a.m. or after 9:00 p.m. local (to them). Don't call or text people on the DNC (either the national registry or your own list). Don't ever call or text using an autodialer or pre-recorded message unless you've got prior express written consent – either for marketing or informational purposes.

Choose Carefully

Remember that the courts will hold your company responsible for violating the TCPA regulations even if you never make a single call… if you hire another firm to make your calls for you. They do it wrong, you pay the price. You'll be what they call "vicariously liable" and on the hook for whatever fines arise from complaints. This means it's never been more important to shop carefully. Before you hire a telemarketing company, it's crucial to have a good, thorough conversation about compliance. Beware of companies that brush this discussion aside or who "guarantee" that they'll take the bullet for you if legal questions arise. There is no viable way for these agencies to protect your company financially from settlement requirements in the multiple millions, no matter what insurance they may claim to carry.

What's on the Compliance Horizon?

In mid-2018, marketers worldwide scrambled to figure out what the European Union's General Data Protection Regulation (GDPR) meant for them. Every company with a website – from mommy bloggers up to industry giants – either found their way into compliance or opted to take a gamble that they were safe because they didn't do business in the EU.

That particular bit of legislation largely covers the acquisition, storage, and use of data among EU citizens. It may or may not extend to the United States and to telemarketing in particular, sooner or later. Vague, for sure, but it's a matter that you'll want to watch.

Likewise, there's the Data Care Act, Consumer Data Protection Act, and legislation proposed by organizations such as the Center for Democracy & Technology to keep an eye on going forward. With the increased frequency of data breaches happening, the public is clamoring for better protection. Lawmakers are listening, to some extent, and while the details of what's coming down the compliance pike are uncertain, compliance isn't going to get easier with time. Stay tuned and stay safe.

Professional Plaintiffs

"Why work, when I can just sue people instead?" Thankfully, this is not the mindset most people hold. But there are always folks who'd rather litigate than work. The TCPA, in particular, looks like just the gravy train some litigious people have been waiting for – and you do not want your company to pay their fare.

While our goal is not to scare the pants off of you as you read this book, it would do you no favors to sugarcoat the risk of non-compliance. If your company makes telemarketing calls, it's a sure bet that someone out there is waiting, watching, and hoping you'll make a non-compliant call. More accurately, they're hoping you'll make multiple non-compliant calls to them. Dollar signs in their eyes, they'd love nothing better than for your call center's error to fund their retirement in Fiji.

Some notable cases:

- One Tennessee man stockpiled phone numbers that had been reassigned and waited for them to ring. One home security company fell into his trap. He filled out a survey and met with one of their installers – just to find out who to sue for calling him on that number without his prior express written consent.
- Another plaintiff filed nearly thirty TCPA actions across the country, engaging with companies and quickly terminating service, then hoping they'd make a non-compliant call to him so he could cash in on their oversight.
- A woman in Pennsylvania accumulated 35 prepaid cell phones to use in her professional plaintiff scheme. Her vigilant documentation of sales calls resulted in a string of lawsuits and pre-litigation demand letters, always with the claim that these companies had violated the TCPA. She actually admitted in her testimony that her plan was to manufacture lawsuits. So far, she's had a hard time proving "concrete injury" in court, but the companies she's sued know that even defending a failed lawsuit is expensive.

While it is true that anyone, anywhere can sue your company for anything, the goal is to minimize that risk – and to do business in such a way that a professional plaintiff's case will fall apart under examination. In addition to doing whatever it takes to ensure TCPA compliance in your call center (including only working with telemarketing partners you trust), some measures you might want to consider include:

- Avoid purchasing lists from off-shore vendors. Not only is it nearly impossible to know with any certainty that the leads you're buying were obtained in a compliant manner, it would be incredibly difficult to take any sort of legal recourse.
- Consider scrubbing your list against a list of TCPA professional plaintiffs. Don't just scrub once; like weeds in a garden bed, these folks are likely to re-emerge regularly.
- Pay attention to how people interact with your business. Are they signing up to get information, then immediately saying, "Stop" or asking to be added to your DNC? The next step they take may be to sue you for subsequent calls.
- Invest in whatever technology you need to remove consumers from your list immediately when they ask to be added to your DNC.
- If your company has multiple call centers across the country, be certain that a DNC request made in one center carries through to all the other call centers so that nobody dials that number again.

- When a consumer asks to be put on your DNC, make sure you get ALL of their phone numbers to add to the list. This way, you can be sure you don't accidentally call their landline when their initial DNC request was connected to their mobile number.
- You might even want to block those DNC numbers forever, meaning if that professional plaintiff tries to sign up again with that same phone number, it'll be blocked. This doesn't preclude the consumer from doing business with you in the future, but it will protect you from the repercussions of calling them with an autodialer.
- Make sure any name associated with a professional plaintiff is blocked from entering your dialing system in the first place. Search and scrub.
- Never use any kind of technology that specifically violates the DNC, TCPA, or GDPR.
- Consult with a TCPA attorney who can make a detailed examination of your processes and procedures and advise you of holes that leave your company vulnerable. Implement whatever changes they recommend.

All these regulations are a pain, of course. They make doing an already hard job way harder. But the people have spoken, and the law is the law. As a consumer, you can probably appreciate the benefits that come from having these rules in place. As someone whose livelihood depends on telemarketing, though, compliance matters are just one more hoop to jump through on the way to making a living.

The stakes are high in the matter of compliance. Fortunately, this is one challenge to profits that you can meet and beat with a mix of getting and following expert legal advice and ongoing vigilance. As they say, an ounce of prevention beats a pound of cure.

Next up, we'll look at another challenge call center managers do battle with in their quest for greater conversions – the quality of the calls they buy.

CHAPTER 5

QUALITY MATTERS

"It is a fundamental fact that no cook, however creative and capable, can produce a dish of a quality any higher than that of its raw ingredients."

Alice Waters

Ever heard of the Project Management Triangle in software development? It goes something like this: "Fast, good, or cheap. Pick two." It speaks to the three-way teeter-totter that comes into play anytime you need to strike a delicate balance between desirable traits that seem to be in opposition to one another.

Business development managers get it. They're trying to balance compliance, quality, and cost per acquisition while getting your sales team the volume of calls needed to make enough sales to hit their numbers.

High-quality leads are typically more expensive than their lower-quality cousins… at least upfront and on paper. Taken in a broader perspective, though, high quality leads convert better and ultimately lead to a lower CPA. It's just like how cooking with better ingredients (assuming the same level of skill in the cook) results in a better meal.

Stock the kitchen with top-grade ingredients but staff it with someone who uses the smoke detector to signal that dinner's ready, however, and the results will probably be awful. Likewise, in your call center, you've got to have high-quality leads AND highly-skilled agents to create the results you want. The skill level of your agents is on you – that's largely about your company's hiring and training processes. But the quality of the leads coming in boils down to how well you choose your performance marketing partner, and ultimately their access to top-notch publishers who will send great leads.

Bad Quality Leads Leave a Bad Taste in Your Mouth (and Worse)

Just like busy families getting takeout so they can skip time-consuming meal preparation, it's no mystery why companies go looking for outsourced lead generation solutions when it's time to scale. The prospect of bypassing the expense of testing and going directly to the part where they talk with prospects is appealing.

In theory, this seems like an ideal way to mitigate marketing risks. In practice, just as you'd feel queasy contemplating ordering out from any place where you've gotten food poisoning, a smart choice boils down to trust. It's crucial that you be able to trust your performance marketing partner - especially in light of the strict regulations governing lead generation and telemarketing, as we just discussed.

Unfortunately, not every leads source is ethical about providing calls that are both fully compliant and high quality. Lead generation can be rather lucrative, and unscrupulous providers believe they can beat the system. They are ever on the lookout for cheap ways to generate leads, legal or otherwise. While they certainly understand that delivering fraudulent and non-compliant calls endangers them and their clients, they are willing to take that risk. By the time they are found out and shut down, they've already been paid. The ill-gotten gain in hand, they lay low for a while, then reopen under a new business name.

Word to the Wise: Find a Trustworthy Source of Leads

Bill Cox, VP Performance Marketing for HolaDoctor, said it well:

"There is a lot you can learn from someone's approach and the way they conduct themselves even on test calls. I like to think the people I work with are respectable people, but I think at the same time in this wild west, it's easy to get burned from time to time."

Are these fraudsters short-sighted? Of course. Most criminal schemes are. These people could just as easily apply their cunning to doing business above-board, building long-term client relationships that benefit everyone involved. But instead, they are in it for the quick buck, caring nothing about the ripple effect of their greed.

With Performance Marketing, It's Like Getting to Sniff the Cork First

You could gamble on whether your campaign will yield quality leads - or you could shift that gamble onto the plate of your performance marketing partner and only pay for leads that meet your quality standards. The arrangement is simple. You bypass the risks involved in testing. You know in advance precisely what you'll pay for every qualified lead.

Then, like smelling the cork before committing to a bottle of wine, every time the phone rings, you typically have a 1-2 minute duration period in which to make the final determination on whether it's up to snuff. End the call before that duration period ends, and you don't pay. No longer are you reaching into a grab bag, blindfolded;

you're now only spending call center resources on the leads that are ripe and ready.

Companies that work with true performance-based lead generation experts recognize the practically miraculous nature of what this arrangement yields.

- They skip past the expensive process of testing and lead generation, jumping right to the point where their agents are on the phone with ready buyers.

- They don't pay for unqualified calls, thus driving their CPA down.

- As they work with their performance marketing partner long-term, they gather more reliable benchmark data, making accurate forecasting easier.

Commercial Intent Matters

With the sweeping takeover of digital, experts and laypeople alike assume that old-fashioned phone calls went the way of the dinosaur. Why pick up the phone and talk when you could fill out a form, click through a social media feed or buy online? In response, small and medium-sized businesses have turned their attention from call leads – a once time-honored method of marketing – to more automated sales methods.

The problem with this is simple: Calling works. By ditching it, you're ditching one of the most effective marketing strategies on the market today. In fact, its effectiveness is growing: According to Sales Hacker, the average call time in January 2016 was 119 seconds, but that time leaped to 254 seconds in January 2017. That's a call time increase of more than 100 percent in a single year, indicating that people may feel some digital fatigue. It seems prospects are more interested in that traditional face-to-face.

Moreover, research indicates that calls have between 30 and 50 percent conversion rates. Compare that to conversion rates for Facebook ads, where the customer clicks the ad and buys online. Those offer a return on only 9 percent of ads placed. Pretty crazy, right? At a bare minimum, call leads give you three times the results of Facebook.

That's not to say online advertising isn't useful. It is the foundation of inbound call generation. This merely indicates that when you take your advertising to the next step, you do better. That's pretty much true any time you extend your funnel. It's especially true when your funnel addition has as much power as phone calls.

Let's take a look at that power. We'll explore who the audience consists of and how inbound call leads work. We will also discuss the power of qualified call leads and how to get the best ones. Lastly, we will take a look at what your ad creative needs to consist of, why mobile matters for getting qualified leads and how to get help today.

Who You Gonna Call?

Typically, inbound call leads consist of consumers. These are people you can convert over the course of a phone call. Unlike businesses, which have to undergo lengthy discussions before they decide to purchase, consumers often convert in a few minutes. This is especially true once they're already qualified with good advertising (explained below).

Also, typically, your call leads have a more significant decision to make. If your prospect is going to buy a sweater, for instance, there's not much discussion involved. However, if they're going to sign up for an insurance policy, they want to know more. They need details: coverage benefits, premiums, out-of-pocket costs.

That's where a call comes in. It's particularly useful when a prospect truly needs a live conversation before they make a buying decision. Most consumers won't plunk down money until they've had their emotional needs met and their questions answered. Many industries involve an extremely high level of trust before a prospect will convert. Just a few examples:

- Insurance policies

- Legal services

- Medical and dental services

87

- Addiction or psychiatric treatment

- Final expense plans

- Credit repair

- Water damage services

Note that a conversion doesn't have to result in money immediately. In some cases, a conversion means booking an appointment. For instance, a medical center wants people to come in for diagnoses of various health problems, for which they may offer surgery or regimens. An addiction center wants people to join on an inpatient basis or start coming on an outpatient basis. An attorney wants people to schedule a phone consultation to assess whether they can help.

At the end of the day, your audience consists of primary decision-makers. At most, they have to discuss their decision with a spouse or parent. They have a problem, they learn you can solve it, and they have the power to convert in the moment.

The Inbound Call Generation Process

As stated, most inbound call generation is set up for B2C companies. Those are the ones geared toward selling directly to individuals. So, say you're working for an addiction treatment center. Your inbound call process would look like this:

- Contract with an inbound marketing center to handle your phone calls

- Post an ad on Facebook explaining who you are and what you offer

- The call center waits for customers to call

- The call center picks up the phone and explains the offer

- They get rerouted by the call center once they're ready to buy

The result? You pay per call, but only pick up your own phone when prospects have said they would like to move forward with a treatment plan. This saves your team time and money.

On the phone with you, they not only get their questions answered. They also feel heard. It gives them a sense that someone is looking out for them. And it increases the know-like-trust factor, which is critical in conversions. Until prospects know you, they won't call. (That's where ads come in.) Until they like you, they won't move forward. (That's where the call center comes in.) Once they trust you, they will buy. (That's where your team comes in, making the final sale.)

This know-like-trust power is critical. It helps you weed out those who aren't serious at every level. So how exactly does that work, and why does it matter?

Inbound Beats Cold, Hands-Down

One of the most potent benefits of inbound call generation is the quality of the leads. To see why this is so, let's compare inbound call leads to cold call leads.

With the latter, you buy a list of leads who generally fit your audience profile. If you sell life insurance, for instance, young and middle-aged parents are your target. You then call those people, hoping to schedule a meeting. Most refuse if they even pick up. Of those you do convince to meet with you, many will cancel or reject you at the meeting. Only a few will convert. Estimates of cold call conversion rates clock in around two percent. That's nothing compared to the 30 or 50 percent we saw above and makes truly poor use of your time – and your team's.

On the other hand, inbound call leads hit that 30-50 mark, giving you 15 to 25 times the returns on cold calling. Your team only devotes time to leads once they've passed a two-tiered benchmark: they've clicked on an ad, and they've spoken to a call center representative. This not only eliminates the need for cold calling; it also eliminates a lot of people who might otherwise call without serious intent. That includes:

- Price shoppers, who are only looking for the lowest possible price and don't actually care about the value you bring to the table

- Uneducated shoppers, who have made no effort to understand your product or market, and want you to explain it to them from the ground up

- Resentful shoppers, who hate that they have to spend the money and want to argue you down on price or dispute the value of your products and services

- Non-shoppers or competitors, who only want to keep you on the phone long enough to learn the trade or market and make use of it for their own ends

- Disinterested parties, who don't know they're disinterested until they get you on the phone and pick your brain

All of these people are a horrible time suck. Too often, though, businesses get sucked into talking with them in an effort to convert. That's a clear warning sign that you've got a quality issue.

Again, qualified call leads exhibit none of these qualities. With a call center acting as the gatekeeper, you only get leads once they've read your ad, called the center and spent several minutes on the phone with a representative who isn't you. Because the call center has scalability on their side, they can offer much better rates to you for those minutes on the phone than you can provide to your own employees, saving you money and keeping their time sacred.

All of this only works, of course, if you have great ad creative.

What Should Your Advertising Creative Include?

To generate call leads with high commercial intent, you need good ad creative. If yours is unclear, milquetoast or off-putting, the call center won't get leads. That means they'll never get to you. As such, you need compelling content that sucks your reader in.

Foundationally, your advertising needs to include the same essential characteristics of any type of marketing, including:

- A clear statement of who you are

- Which services you provide to your customers

- The benefits they can expect to get

- What happens when they get in touch with you

- A time period

In the above example of a treatment center, for instance, your ad must state that you are an addiction center. You should say that you provide treatments (either general or 12-step, for example). You should include benefits – sobriety, health, happiness, family ties. Then explain what happens when they call, such as talking to a real individual and making an intake appointment. Then the time period: Today? Tomorrow? Next week?

In this example, time is obviously of the essence. Addiction is dangerous. Overdoses happen all the time. So, your ad might include a promise that "confidential, compassionate help is just a phone call away" and a call-to-action to "call now."

Don't Skimp on a Strong Mobile Presence

According to Marketing Land, clicks have dismal rates of return. Conversions "top out" at 1 or 2 percent for online advertising, as opposed to upwards of 50 percent. And mobile is king among those conversions.

Of the top phone call sources, 16 percent of calls come from offline channels, while 30 percent come from non-mobile online channels. A full 54 percent, however, come from mobile-only channels, indicating that you need a strong mobile presence to succeed. That means, in turn, that you need a marketing company that can set up an effective conversion funnel beginning with mobile ads and routing through a call center, before finally arriving at your telephonic doorstep.

If you consider the buying cycle – awareness, consideration, purchase – then it's critical you appear on mobile. That's where most people do their searches, for local and non-local services alike. If you don't show up there, you have entirely skipped the "awareness" step. Needless to say, it's pretty important that people know about you, or they can't possibly get in touch.

One extra advantage of mobile is that your calls-to-action can link directly to phone numbers that callers simply have to click. Voilà: they're in touch with your call center, and shortly afterward in contact with you. That's not to say you don't need a desktop version as well, because you do. This merely means if you don't have a mobile presence, you're missing out – so make sure the marketing company with whom you work has a thorough understanding of both platforms.

Insider Tips for Getting the Best Quality at the Best Price

The biggest mistake you could make in getting more calls coming in would be to price-shop. The second biggest would be to buy without having a conversation with the call source you're considering. The goal should not be jumping on a bargain like it's a nice set of kitchen knives on special through a clearance site. Ultimately, you'll save money and get the best results when you establish an ongoing relationship with a call provider who'll invest the time in listening and learning what you need. Get one who'll grow with you, and you can get what you need without having to go through the search process over and over.

Here are some tips to help you buy well right out of the gate:

- **Decide whether you want on-shore or off-shore.** There are benefits to both, but with off-shore providers, the list is very short, including only "low price" if we're going to be completely honest. How'd they generate these leads? Are these calls compliant? Are you certain enough to put money on that gamble?

  With on-shore providers, the benefit list is quite a bit more extensive. You can require proof of prior express written consent and get it. Jornaya and TrustedForm, as we've mentioned before, are two ways to get documentation of the very moment a prospect gave consent. If your call provider will also talk with your prospects, you'd better believe the advantage goes to stateside call centers. There's nothing that'll sink your success rate faster than making your prospects talk with overseas agents whose first language is not English. Beyond the language barrier, a lot also gets lost in translation when you account for cultural and idiomatic differences. Is it worth losing all the benefits of a more controlled and near-seamless call process on-shore just to get a better price?

- **Opponents or partners? You choose.** Don't fall prey to a mindset in which it's a dog-eat-dog world where you've got to look out for #1 at all costs. That might work on Wall Street in the pit of the NYSE, but it's no way to engage in business long-term. Business is business, of course, but you'll get much better results from working with a lead provider you can cooperate with than one with whom you're always trying to get the upper hand.

  In fact, the best providers see the relationship as a partnership that's mutually beneficial. They're not trying to squeeze you for every dollar; they're trying to help you succeed because they realize when they help you succeed, it pays off for them, too. With that in mind, understand that purchasing calls and leads is very much a two-way street. Be honest and transparent rather than playing games. An integrity-driven provider plays by those rules, too, and will value the opportunity to help a fellow "good guy" win.

- **High-tech or two cans on a string?** Generating calls, clicks, and leads in an online age means a whole lot of technological moving parts. That stuff isn't cheap; but it does have a major impact on the results. Seek a partner that invests heavily in the tech required to do a stellar job, even though there may be vendors who promise the same results at half the price using yesterday's technology.

In the end, where quality is concerned, it truly is a matter of garbage in, garbage out. The quality of the calls, clicks, and leads you have to work with will absolutely determine how likely you are to hit your numbers.

In some fields that require high-priced tools or equipment, they say, "buy once, cry once," meaning it's better to spend more on quality than to skimp and end up with inferior results. Keep this in mind where the quality of your calls is concerned.

There's one more ball you'll need to keep your eye on to get the best results from your call center. Next up, we'll look at your numbers.

CHAPTER 6

IS YOUR CPA TOO HIGH, TOO LOW, OR JUST RIGHT?

"Do not worry too much about your difficulty in mathematics, I can assure you that mine are still greater."

Albert Einstein

Remember when we were kids? If you wanted to paint a picture, and not just stick figures and the outline of a house, your best bet was to get a paint by number kit. Of course, the resulting objet d'art never really came out looking like the picture on the box. Gracious parents everywhere have refrigerators bedecked with magnets holding such masterpieces in place.

99

Numbers might not be enough to turn middle-schoolers into Monet. But if nothing else, some of us learned that numbers are our friends – helpful guides that can usher us toward a result we want. For others, the combination of paint by number disappointment and seventh-grade math class word problem torture was enough to put us off of math forever.

Love numbers or hate them, if you're in this business, they play a huge role in your work life. If that's true about numbers, it goes double for acronyms. Combine the two and it's no wonder nobody really wants to hear about your job when you're out with friends.

But here, we get it. We're just as hung up on numbers as you probably are. Maybe even more so, because not only do we watch our own numbers... we watch our clients' numbers as well.

One challenge we've been surprised to see stymie some call buyers is their wrestling match with key performance indicators (KPIs) that leave them hobbled instead of celebrating yet another quarter in which sales figures surpassed projections. In talking with some of the experts who've weighed in on the contents of this book, we see we're not alone in having our eyebrows raised here. There are two angles to this perplexity:

1. Sometimes, call centers chase management-chosen numbers that don't serve them.

2. Sometimes, it's hard to know which metrics matter in the first place, and which are irrelevant.

Across the board, though, CPA is one number that can be unpacked well enough to provide value. Boiled down, CPA speaks to how much your company can afford to spend to make new customers. If it costs you a dollar to get a new customer who brings in a profit of $3, you'd make that trade all day long. Reverse those numbers and get only $1 after spending $3 to land that new customer, and you've got a problem.

Put that simply, CPA is a piece of cake.

But once that piece of cake meets with the rigors of reality, it can be harder to calculate – and harder to apply to your marketing budget. We dug into this fuzzy math topic at length with Bill Cox of Hola Doctor. Here's how he describes the difference between raw and billable calls, and how CPA is not always what it seems:

"Some call providers might try to send me 100 calls but maybe we can only answer 75 of them. Of those 75, maybe we disqualify 50%. An upfront agreement to pay $50 per call might sound great on the surface but if we're only accepting 50% of the calls they send us, my effective revenue per call to that supplier is half of that… just $25."

The math gets much more complicated for business development managers who decide to start their lead acquisition strategy much higher in the funnel. Now, you're not just crunching numbers based on phone calls purchased vs. taken vs. closed.

Instead, now maybe you're buying data. You're constructing and testing your own funnel, building your own forms, and waiting for the phone to ring. There's a lot more complexity in the math the further you move upward from the funnel milestone in which prospects call you. Rather than looking at what you paid for each call, whether it converted, and the customer value you just brought in, you've got to watch many other numbers as well, covering the whole process of funnel creation, promotion, and testing.

The Most Complicated Machine Possible

To put it much more simply, let's say you want help moving a book from your shelf to your desk (except you want to do this thousands of times a day... and your livelihood depends on the results).

Buying calls is like paying someone to come in, reach up to grab the book, walk a few steps to your desk, and lay the book down. Easy. Easy to do, easy to determine whether it was done, and easy to calculate whether it makes sense to continue paying for this arrangement.

But the higher you move upward in the sales funnel, the more complicated, risky, and expensive the process becomes. In fact, the process starts to look like a Rube Goldberg machine. DigitalTrends.com describes these hypnotic, impractical machines like this:

"Complicated, deliberately over-engineered contraptions that ultimately perform a very simple task… One step triggers the next in a chain reaction until the final task is complete. Once it starts, it's practically impossible to peel yourself away from the anticipation of what's coming next."

(https://www.digitaltrends.com/cool-tech-best-rube-goldberg-machines)

Obviously, the more of the funnel you can build in-house… assuming you optimize the living daylights out of it so that it works like a cash machine, theoretically, the better. Conceptually, generating all your leads internally should be the most economical option. The reality is, it can be the most expensive way to get new business.

Between the costs of funnel construction, the expenses involved in testing it, and the high risk of missing the mark, exclusively internally-generated leads that are affordable isn't always practical or even possible. Nice in theory, unicorn-like in reality. The DIY plan is certainly not always financially feasible, especially given the way marketing technology advances by leaps and bounds every other Tuesday these days.

So, Which Numbers Count?

One question we asked the experts we interviewed for this book went something like this, "What KPIs matter most?" It sounded simple enough, but one after another, the answer we got was something like, "It depends." They weren't hedging, of course. The vagueness only mirrors the ambiguity of the question.

Which metrics matter most depends on your organization's goals, of course. But even more, it depends on which part of the funnel you're measuring.

Most marketing students can tell you that the funnel parts, from top to bottom, include customer journey stages such as Awareness, Interest, Evaluation, and Sale. The funnel labels might vary, but the idea is the same. The further into the funnel prospects go, the closer they come to buying. Also, selling B2B is different from selling B2C, despite many commonalities.

- **CTR:** For a company doing all its own heavy lifting, funnel-wise, one of the first significant metrics is the click-through-rate or CTR of your landing pages and any paid ads you run.

- **Conversion Rate:** Now, you're looking at how many people reach a set campaign goal (like filling out a form) once they reach your landing page.

- **Visitors to Lead:** Here, you'll count how many of those visitors who reached that first campaign goal become legitimate leads.

- **Lead to Opportunity:** Now you're looking at how many of those legitimate leads finally end up in the hands of your sales team

- **Opportunities to Wins:** Of those leads who talked with sales, how many made a purchase?

- **Time to Conversion:** Some buying decisions take longer than others, of course. It may be helpful to look at how long your prospects spend in each part of your funnel.

- **ROI:** Obviously a universally important number to watch, this metric lets you know whether what you did paid off, and by how much. As simple as that sounds, it actually gets complicated quickly – especially for complicated funnels. It gets even more complicated when you take into account the average customer lifetime value.

- **CPC:** Cost-per-click becomes really important if you're running your own online ads. The only way to drive a high CPC down is to tweak and optimize your ads and your funnel as a whole.

- **CPM:** Cost-per-mille is relevant for anyone running ads on the display network (either in search engines or social media). It tracks your cost per every thousand impressions.

- **CPL**: Cost per lead speaks to the cost to acquire leads – but it's not a simple number. It varies when you consider the changing cost of buying traffic. It must include the costs of any lead magnets (ebooks or other giveaways). Finally, you've got to include any costs involved in the mechanics of generating leads, like your CRM or email marketing software.

These numbers may or may not figure into your CPA numbers. By buying your calls, you can ignore any costs involved in building the funnel, driving traffic to it, and the testing and tweaking phase. Those costs and risks transfer to your call provider.

In that case, your math gets simpler. Primarily, you're looking at how your investment in these calls performs. As we said before, if you can spend a dollar to get a call that generates $3 in revenue, great. Do that all day!

But It's Not Just about CPA

Some call buyers stumble, short-sighted, right out of the gate. They've bought into a common fallacy that says:

High Compliance + High Quality = High CPA

As Nick Elser says, "There's a lot more that goes into CPA than just your marketing tactics. It's your sales team. It's how you allocate your funds. It's your allocation schedules. It's a lot to do with the type of marketing you're doing. You could be completely compliant in a low-cost campaign spread out over an organic timeframe and be at a very, very reasonable CPA. The real key is making sure the entirety of the organization runs like a well-oiled machine."

Among some of the businesses he's served as a consultant, he's seen many that follow a predictable path that takes them off-course. "They find a tactic that works for them. They see revenue coming in. But their funnel is leaky. There's data that could be monetized but is left sitting on the table. There are holes in their sales infrastructure and process. There are holes in their accounts receivable." These holes are overlooked because, despite them, the business is making money. Bills are getting paid. Profits are being reaped. They get complacent. Rather than optimizing at each step in their funnel, they're coasting.

Add Compliance and Quality to the Equation

When compliance regulations reproduce like rabbits, business development managers who've been coasting along are left high and dry and out of practice when it comes to adapting. All of a sudden, profit margins plunge, and the pressure is on for them to find a new way to generate new business.

The bigger problem that comes next is the way this change of fortune forces a BDM's hand. With the rug ripped out from under their feet, the urgency level gets dialed way up. They need to find new business NOW, and they might hear murmurs of high stakes regarding low CPAs. In near-panic mode, it might be tempting to overlook red flags and fall prey to unscrupulous call and lead providers. Their commitment to compliance won't exactly go out the window, but the quest for low CPAs might leave them willing to take more risks – actively or passively – than they did when everything was rosy.

Weigh the True Cost of Your Leads

Focusing only on low CPA is like taking a "shortcut" through a bad part of town driving a car that stalls out every few yards. Not a great plan, to say the least. While it's basic business wisdom that your company needs a reliable way to bring in new customers at a profit, and to have multiple ways to do that, reason sometimes goes out the window. When that happens, it's easy to wind up in trouble.

In the end, winning the numbers game isn't as simple as doing some simple math. What good is a low CPA if you end up parrying a professional plaintiff who slipped through because those cheap calls weren't exactly compliant? What good is it to buy a truckload of cheap leads your call center can't close because the quality of those leads was terrible?

Don't look at your CPA in a vacuum. Spend what makes sense to get leads that convert at rates that pale in comparison with the ongoing value of those new customers.

Maybe you've got all of these challenges – compliance, quality, and cost – mastered. If so, there's really no limit on how far you can surpass this year's sales goals. But if not, you may have some decisions to make as you get your house in order and prepare to scale for real. Next, we're going to give you some easy ways you can get the calls, clicks, and leads you need – from a performance marketing partner you'll want to keep around long-term.

CHAPTER 7

EENY MEENY MINY MOE – CHOOSE YOUR PARTNER WISELY

"It is not hard to make decisions when you know what your values are."

Roy Disney

As kids, we had a highly-respected if not particularly discriminating tactic for choosing who was going to be on our team for a game of kickball.

Eeny, meeny, miny, moe
Catch a tiger by the toe
If he hollers, let him go
My mother says to pick
The very best one
And you are
It.

There's your teammate, right at the end of your pointy little finger. It was universally accepted that this rhyme was the boss. Whine or argue with the results, and you risked being taunted with cries of, "Cheater, cheater pumpkin eater!"

If only making business decisions were that simple. The stakes are higher, though, so it makes sense that doing due diligence is the norm when it comes to choosing where you'll acquire your calls and leads.

We asked Bill Cox what advice he'd give a call center owner or manager about choosing a call provider or affiliate network, and it was clear he's been through this buying process a few times and seen the good, the bad, and the ugly.

"The affiliate space can feel a bit like the wild west. The barriers to entry are pretty low. Literally, anyone could go out there and create www.myrandominsurancesite. com. They could create their own brand and send traffic to it, then find a buyer who'll purchase their leads – and they can do it all really quickly. They'd go the "turn and burn" route, sending a ton of fraudulent traffic to their buyers."

Hopefully, the buyer would realize what was going on quickly and shut that provider down. But it's possible the provider would send a mix of good quality calls among the bad, trying to disguise the truth of what's happening. In that case, it might take longer to realize what's going on and to pull the plug on it.

Start Asking Basic Questions

To be completely honest, choosing your call provider somewhat boils down to a gut feeling. Just a few minutes into your initial conversation, you'll have a feeling one way or the other as to whether this is someone you trust. That's important intel to heed. But while you can easily eliminate some based on the sense that something's not quite right, you're not ready yet to make a buying decision. You've got to have further conversation.

It's never been so important to do some extensive vetting with any call or lead supplier you consider engaging. At a minimum, you should ask questions about:

- How long they've been in business

- How many employees they have

- How much revenue they do

- Which vertical(s) they work in

- What traffic methods they use – and can they provide evidence of the sites they're sending traffic to

Above-board lead sellers should be willing to reveal that information. The shady ones will certainly be hesitant to provide even that basic transparency.

Ramp Up Your Questions to Dive Deeper

Assuming an affiliate network or broker passes muster in your initial conversations by answering your questions to your liking, it's now time to dig a little deeper rather than taking them on face-value. You'll want to zoom in closer by asking questions that help you suss out what to expect regarding:

- **How deep is the well?** How long can they keep up with your needs? The whole reason you're having conversations with performance marketers is that your company can only generate so many leads in-house. The need can escalate quickly… 50 leads this week can turn into 100, 200, 400 or even thousands in just a few weeks. Just as you might hit the wall when you try to scale, a call provider might, too. When your well dried up, you went looking for a new source. They're likely to do the same. How will this partner you're vetting deal with that challenge? Will they tell you they're tapped out? Or, will they reach out to other providers who may or may not share their (or your) values and sensitivity to compliance matters.

- **Do they taste test before they serve?** It's ideal to work with a broker who listens to call recordings to spot check how their publishers are doing. No doubt, they've got some publishers they've been working with for years and they've come to trust them. They should still listen in on random recordings now and then to make sure their publishers are still toeing the line rather than veering off into problem areas. It's just as important for your partners to have procedures in place for vetting new publishers. Do they take just anyone who applies as an affiliate? Or are they known in the industry for new publishers finding it very hard to get approved?

- **What information would they find helpful from you?** A great partner not only understands the numbers relevant to their business; they also understand the numbers relevant to yours. This kind of partner can take certain metrics from you and use them to optimize the calls they send you. Knowing what's working makes it easier to replicate good results. From data you can provide, your partner can identify which of their publishers are producing the calls your team is most likely to close – and send more of them.

- **What's their blacklist like?** Anyone in charge of purchasing soon develops preferences for certain vendors. Likewise, everyone keeps a blacklist, vendors they'll never do business with again. It's the same with call providers and publishers. This industry is a small world; some would even say it's incestuous. The same publisher who gets banned on one affiliate network today will apply to ten more tomorrow. Call providers talk. You want one who keeps track of the bad apples and maintains vigilance to keep them from sneaking in.

- **Ask about compliance, then let them talk.** If your understanding about compliance matters is solid, you'll be able to spot someone who's faking their knowledge in this area. Ask open-ended questions to find out how much they understand, how dedicated to compliance they are, and how confidently they can vouch for the compliance of the calls and leads they're selling.

Do Your Homework

This is the time to whip out any sleuthing skills you've got. It's crucial for you to know who you're dealing with before you sign on the dotted line. Ask around and get referrals from other business development managers. Learn as much as you can so that you know what you should expect.

If It Sounds Too Good to Be True…

It's a vulnerable spot you're in as a buyer. The whole reason you're in the market for calls is that it doesn't make sense to try generating enough on your own. You wouldn't be shopping if you didn't have a need to fill. While some call providers want nothing more than to help you succeed, others see nothing but a target on your forehead… their next meal. Just as in the used-car business, it's commonly known that the car that was "only ever driven to church on Sundays by a little old lady" is bunk, you'll soon get good at recognizing when someone's trying to snow you about the calls they can provide. If what they're promising sounds too good to be true, it probably is.

Trust but Indemnify

No matter how good a compliance game a potential lead gen partner may talk, there's no way you can be completely sure they're doing it right, unfortunately. If you remember from our discussion about compliance, the courts see you and your telemarketing partner as equally culpable if there's any funny business going on. This is why it's especially important to engage an experienced attorney as you draw up the paperwork.

Be sure to include an indemnity clause. It's not a bulletproof vest, but it will help protect you if things go south. As Matt Loker says, "If litigation occurs, this clause would force the person who caused the violation

– whether it's the actual caller or the lead supplier – to pay your defense costs and pay any damages you incur as a result, which would be your settlement or your verdict. That will ensure that your business doesn't go out of business because of someone else's illegal conduct." Of course, having an indemnity clause doesn't guarantee the other party will live up to their obligations in the face of a settlement demand. But companies willing to furnish this kind of assurance – and to provide proof of their own insurance – are more likely to have a track record of legitimacy.

Go Slow, Grow Safely

The wise path forward with a new call provider is to start off slowly with a small budget. See how they do. If it's working, scale it up just a little bit. Avoid the urge to ramp up too quickly – even with a good provider, quality can suffer if you try to go too high too fast.

Seeking a Mutually Beneficial Long-Term Relationship?

It's best to take a long-term approach in your search for a performance marketing partner. You want the benefits of scalability without the steep downside inherent in testing. But you also recognize that low CPA means nothing in light of the penalties that accompany non-compliance with DNC, TCPA, and the upcoming GDPR law expansion.

At Digital Market Media, our long track record also allows us to bring both experience and intel to the table. There are lots of affiliates out there who produce low-quality, non-compliant, fraudulent calls. We know them. We watch them. We participate in an alliance of performance marketing networks. There, we help one another by sharing this sort of information - information our clients don't have access to on their own.

In fact, we can perform checks in a few seconds where it might be impossible for an advertiser to ever get to that level of intel. Put into dollars and cents, our longevity in the industry delivers considerable savings to our clients.

By placing such high value on long-term relationships with our clients, we're also able to grow with them. Like becoming a 'regular' at your favorite restaurant, the fit gets even better over time as we learn more about our clients' preferences, CPAs, and results. We understand fully that it's in our mutual best interest to send only top-quality, fully-compliant calls their way. It's this commitment to protecting and providing for our clients - even to our own detriment, at times - that drives us.

Cash In On Our Investments in Technology

When you partner with Digital Market Media, you also get the benefit of our massive investment in testing and technology. Since 2001, we have invested millions and millions of dollars testing various advertising mediums and platforms in multiple verticals. Quite simply, we know how to reach your prospects and draw them in at just the right moment in their buying journey.

Our clients benefit from shifting that risk to us, their pay per call partners. Instead of investing in in-house testing, they pay only for the net result of their partners' testing and toil. Now, every call that reaches the call center has a dramatically better chance of conversion.

At Digital Market Media, our exceptionally creative marketing team works very hard to generate very high-quality leads and calls. We employ the latest marketing techniques, work with high-quality publishers, and focus on compliance with every call. This ensures that our clients have the best possible experience, reach the lowest possible cost to acquire new sales, and achieve a great return on their investment.

Our leads all come with either a Jornaya Lead ID or a Trusted Form certificate. Both Jornaya and Trusted Form serve to capture the moment when a consumer fills out one of our web forms, capturing the consumer's IP address and date stamping the interaction.

Just a Couple of Our Delighted Clients

Gathering testimonials is a tricky business in this business! At least if they're published where anyone can find them. Of course, every single repeat order we get from our clients serves as lovely validation that they appreciate and value what we provide. Then, there are the regular conversations we have, during which we hear them sing our praises, which feels wonderful.

But when it comes to asking our advertisers to provide an official testimonial we can publish, that's when we get cold feet. Not because we don't know they'll shout from the mountaintops about how we help them. Our hesitation comes from wanting to watch out for THEM. See, if you're crushing it in, say, final expense insurance, and a huge part of your success stems from getting top-notch calls from us, what happens when you publicize that fact? Your competitors' ears perk up. Next thing, they're calling us, too. Understandable.

But it goes further than that. Every call provider out there with half a brain and a finger on the pulse of the market now knows that you buy leads. They'd be stupid not to call you to try to pitch you, promising you the world. Not only would that waste your time and bandwidth, fending off a flood of calls, it might also lead to disaster if a less scrupulous provider lured you into the dark side.

That said, we're honored to share Bill Cox and Nick Elser's feedback regarding their experience using our services. They said it's okay.

Bill Cox says, *"When I first started at a company where I increased their call volume from 0-2500 calls a day, it was done largely on the shoulders of Digital Market Media. Tom kind of took me by the hand and explained something you don't expect a supplier to explain very often. That was that I was paying for more calls than I needed to. He told me, 'You need to disqualify these calls quicker.' That's feedback you wouldn't expect a supplier to provide because it's telling me to pay them less. But the goal there is, we want to make this long-term, and if you can't get [maximum value] we're not going to have you keep over-buying. Instead, Tom wanted to help me figure out how to scale, say from 50,000 a month to 50,000 calls a week. He was most interested in getting the calls working for our center. That's what an affiliate is supposed to do; it's supposed to be an extension of your business and work with you to build a model that works. You find the right affiliate, and there's no reason [your relationship] can't exist indefinitely."*

Nick Elser says, *"Tom and Angela are phenomenal people to work with, and what I appreciate most is their transparency. Tom has never once told me he could do something and not done it. He's never told me he couldn't do something and tried to sell it to me anyway. He's always told me, 'Nick, I don't think that's going to work.' Or, 'Nick, this is what I've got right now.' He's always been straightforward with me. He's always worked with me on pricing. I've never, never had a problem. Doing good business is more important than having a good product, because you can always develop better products. You can't teach an old dog new tricks when it comes to doing bad business."*

Top-Quality, Compliant, Affordable Leads Served on a Silver Platter

With broad experience in 25 different verticals, we know what's working in lead generation. We can cross-reference our data to make sound recommendations about which medium is most apt to work for any specific market.

By working with a pay per performance partner like Digital Market Media, there's no need to invest in the team, technology, or testing required to bring lead generation in-house. You simply request the call volume you want to start with and increase it once you're delighted with the results.

But our dedication to your complete satisfaction doesn't end when the phone rings. The generous call durations we offer are much like the experience of dining in a fine restaurant. We're so sure you'll find the leads we bring you to your liking that you can essentially eat half the dish before deciding whether you like it. We're confident you will, and that you'll soon ask for seconds.

If you're eager to make the most of your marketing budget by plugging the profit-leaking holes inherent in team-building, technology, and testing in-house campaigns, we'd like to speak with you. Just connect with us online or call us and we'll help you determine the path forward that makes the most sense for your organization.

You can find us here:

www.DigitalMarketMedia.com

888-432-1819

EXPERT RESOURCES

Nicholas Elser of CEO Donnaefinn Consulting is a 33-year-old father of two boys, Finnley and Ari. He made his start consulting after working extensively in sales and in the substance abuse treatment space. After making some disturbing observations of sales procedures in self-proclaimed "successful" companies, he made it his career path to help small companies grow and repair.

Nicholas understands taking on failing companies or dealing with tunnel-visioned ownership is risky, but states, "I never learned how to fail." Proficient in HTML, CSS3, JQUERY, and APEX Class, Nicholas is a Front End Salesforce developer, web designer, and lead generator. With his skill set, Nicholas has consulted with and helped over a dozen companies in his first year of business.

To maximize your revenue, call Donnaefinn Consulting for a free consultation at 561-515-4556. Mention this book and receive a special introductory rate.

Bill Cox, Vice President of Performance Marketing for Hola Doctor, has worked with the largest publicly traded vertical marketing companies, some of the larger life insurance brokerages, and multiple multinational companies entering the US market.

A creative and analytical business leader with an extensive background in digital marketing and campaign management, Bill uses his marketing experience to create products and grow business. He sees his goal as visualizing and conveying the entire life cycle of the products and companies he represents, developing strategies that provide long term success for his clients.

Mark Coudray, Founder of Coudray Growth Technologies, is recognized and awarded internationally as a premiere thought leader and business optimization strategist. His passion in life is finding and developing better ways of doing things and implementing them so others can excel to their full potential. His knowledge has been shared globally in more than 500 published feature articles, columns, research pieces, and white papers.

Since 2006, Mark's activities have expanded beyond the graphic communications industry to include clients in retail, entertainment, medical, call center, education, and industrial sectors. He specializes in the transformation of analog companies so they can prosper and succeed in the digital economy. His primary focus is compressing and accelerating lead generation and sales process automation to position his clients for maximum growth and valuation at the time of exit.

If you feel your business is not operating at its full competitive potential, contact Mark to discuss the specifics of your situation. You can reach him at 805-748-3129.

Matthew M. Loker, Esq., Partner in the Kazerouni Law Group, APC, has been an instrumental litigation attorney on Consumer Rights cases. He's been featured in multiple media interviews and podcasts on this topic, is Professor of Contracts at the San Luis Obispo College of Law, and has a contagious enthusiasm for an area of the law that most people probably don't even know exists.

If you don't already have an attorney who has deep experience in the laws governing telemarketing, one of the smartest moves you could make would be to call Matt at 949-404-4228 to arrange a free consultation.

ABOUT THE AUTHORS

Tom Carolan is an expert in the growing field of pay per call marketing, and the author of *Goliath Is Falling!* and now *Have Them at Hello*. The co-founder of San Luis Obispo, CA-based Digital Market Media, Tom's entrepreneurial career began in the UK.

His first business endeavor, Carolan's Property Services, a company he founded in London, was nominated for "The Best Small Business of the Year Award" from the Prince of Wales Business Trust in December 1993. That business delivered an astounding 1000% return on investment for its venture capital partners. In the US, Tom proved his insurance marketing expertise in over 13 years at Parasol Leads, a company he founded and ultimately sold. As President and CEO, he led the company to the "Best Leads Quality in America" award from the LeadsCouncil in January 2014. In fact, from 2007 until he sold it, Parasol Leads maintained an A+ Rating for Customer Satisfaction from the Better Business Bureau each and every year.

Always evolving, Tom continues to raise the bar in customer expectations as he drives their success into the online marketing world. His mission is ambitious – to lead Digital Market Media to be recognized as the highest-quality lead provider in the industry.

Tom's insatiable hunger for understanding has resulted in a diversified education and the ability to grasp what's most important to learn about any strategy, tactic, or tool useful for marketing. His commitment to serving others shows up in his long list of recommendations from clients and colleagues alike.

Tom's clients benefit from his unrivaled connections, integrity, expertise, and effectiveness. His passion is helping his clients compete better online so they can grow their businesses, benefitting their employees, clients, vendors, networking partners, and communities alike.

Be sure to request your complimentary consultation, an overview of your current lead generation strategy from an unbiased professional. Tom will help you assess what you're doing well, what could use improvement, and some suggestions you can use to get better results.

You can connect with Tom here:
www.digitalmarketmedia.com/contact-us
By phone: 888-432-1819 Ext. 701

Susan Anderson started Triumph Communications, LLC in 2005 upon realizing this Internet thing was here to stay and that there sure was a lot of horrid content already clogging it up. She started off as a solo writer, creating so much highly-rated content for clients that she rose to the top spot on Guru, where she met Tom through some initial writing projects there. Since then, she's built a team of US-based writers to serve a select group of marketing consultants and their clients.

She fell into a bit of a strange specialty – taking businesses most people find dull, complicated, or super-niched, and extracting what's useful, actionable, interesting, and even fascinating about them, then writing about these businesses in a way that actual humans get value from what they read.

Even though she's a bit of a hermit, she's enjoyed presenting online and in-person training on freelance writing as part of Eben Pagan's Traffic School and Ignition programs, Coffee Shop Millionaire, and was even flown to Fiji to teach there.

Susan splits her time between Huntsville, Alabama and the Tri-Cities area of Eastern Tennessee. Mom to two young adults and a small ark's worth of animals, she counts walking on fire and breaking a wooden arrow with her throat as piece-of-cake kinds of accomplishments in comparison. If she's not writing, she's probably taking a long walk with the love of her life, trying to convince her chickens to weed the garden, or wiping drool off of her 1959 Volkswagen Beetle Ragtop, Miss Mabel (built by said love of her life).